ALASTAIR SAWDAY'S

Special
places to stay

LONDON

Edited by Tom Bell

Design: .... Caroline King &
                                              Springboard Design, Bristol

Mapping: .... Springboard Design, Bristol

Maps: .... Bartholomew Mapping Services,
                                              a division of HarperCollins
                                              Publishers, Glasgow

Printing: .... Canale, Italy

UK Distribution: .... Portfolio, Greenford, Middlesex

US Distribution: .... The Globe Pequot Press,
                                              Guilford, Connecticut

Published in June 2002

Alastair Sawday Publishing Co. Ltd
Home Farm Stables, Barrow Gurney, Bristol BS48 3RW
Tel: +44 (0)1275 464891 Fax: +44 (0)1275 464887
E-mail: info@specialplacestostay.com Web: www.specialplacestostay.com

The Globe Pequot Press
P. O. Box 480, Guilford, Connecticut 06437, USA
Tel: +1 203 458 4500 Fax: +1 203 458 4601
E-mail: info@globe-pequot.com Web: www.globe-pequot.com

First edition

Copyright © June 2002 Alastair Sawday Publishing Co. Ltd

A catalogue record for this book is available from the British Library.

ISBN 1-901970-27-2 in the UK

ISBN 0-7627-2458-7 in the US

Printed in Italy

The publishers have made every effort to ensure the accuracy of the information in this
book at the time of going to press. However, they cannot accept any responsibility for
any loss, injury or inconvenience resulting from the use of information contained therein.

ALASTAIR SAWDAY'S

Special

places to stay

Physical Energy, Hyde Park

LONDON

Tonight
With London's ghost
I walk the streets
As easy as November fog
Among the reeds

Patrick Galvin, 'Christ in London'

The
Globe
Pequot
Press

Guilford
Connecticut, USA

Alastair Sawday Publishing
Bristol, UK

Contents

A word from Alastair Sawday

Introduction

General map

Maps

Tube map

South of the River

Henley-on-Thames, New Cross Gate, Brockley, East Dulwich, Crystal Palace, Streatham, Balham, Camberwell, Clapham Common, Battersea

	Entries	Map
Rival	1	6
113 Pepys Road	2	6
57 Breakspears Road	3	6
Shepherd's	4	6
24 Fox Hill	5	6
34 Ambleside Avenue	6	5
38 Killieser Avenue	7	5
108 Streathbourne Road	8	5
The Coach House	9	5
119 Knatchbull Road	10	5
8 Macaulay Road	11	5
22 Northbourne Road	12	5
20 St Philip Street	13	5
Worfield Street	14	5

West, South West

Hampton Court, Richmond, Mortlake, Barnes, Bedford Park, Stamford Brook

Paddock Lodge	15	3
147 Petersham Road	16	3
Doughty Cottage	17	3
Chalon House	18	3

Contents

West, South West (continued)	Entries	Map
131 Queens Road	19	3
The Victoria	20	3
Leyden House	21	3
1 Charlotte Road	22	4
11 Queen Anne's Grove	23	4
7 Emlyn Road	24	4

West Central

Brook Green, Shepherd's Bush, Kensington, Holland Park, Notting Hill, Kensington, Earl's Court, Fulham

31 Rowan Road	25	4
Addison Gardens	26	4
Holland Road	27	4
101 Abbotsbury Road	28	4
Portobello Hotel	29	1
Portobello Gold	30	1
Miller's	31	1
Pembroke Square	32	4
Amsterdam Hotel	33	4
Twenty Nevern Square	34	4
Hartismere Road	35	4
8 Hartismere Road	36	4
29 Winchendon Road	37	4
Crondace Road	38	4
3 Bradbourne Street	39	4
34 Wandsworth Bridge Road	40	4
30 Stokenchurch Street	41	4
8 Parthenia Road	42	4
Barclay Road	43	4
Britannia Road	44	4

Contents

South Central

Chelsea, South Kensington, Pimlico, Sloane Square, Knightsbridge, Victoria, Mayfair, St James's

	Entries	Map
6 Oakfield St	45	4
Old Church Street	46	5
Elm Park Gardens	47	5
Aster House	48	4
Hyde Park Gate	49	4
Imperial College London	50	5
20 Bywater Street	51	5
Number Ninety-Six	52	5
The Sloane Hotel	53	5
The London Outpost	54	5
4 First Street	55	5
Searcy's Roof Garden Bedrooms	56	5
Parkes Hotel	57	5
The Beaufort	58	5
37 Trevor Square	59	5
57 Pont Street	60	5
L'Hotel	61	5
Basil Street Hotel	62	5
16 William Mews	63	5
The Goring	64	5
The Dorchester	65	2
Athenæum Hotel and Apartments	66	2
The Stafford	67	2
22 Jermyn Street	68	2

North Central

Marble Arch, Paddington, Little Venice, Marylebone, Bond Street, Bedford Square, Bloomsbury, Russell Square

Hyde Park Garden Mews	69	2
Norfolk Crescent	70	2
The Colonnade, The Little Venice Town House	71	1
22 York Street	72	2

Contents

North Central (continued)	Entries	Map
Number Ten	73	2
23 Greengarden House	74	2
myhotel Bloomsbury	75	2
The Academy, The Bloomsbury Town House	76	2
University College, London	77	2
The Jenkins Hotel	78	2
The Generator	79	2

North

Hampstead, Primrose Hill, Camden, Highbury, Islington

	Entries	Map
La Gaffe	80	1
Hampstead Village Guest House	81	2
30 King Henry's Road	82	2
78 Albert Street	83	2
66 Camden Square	84	2
4 Highbury Terrace	85	2
26 Florence Street	86	2

www.specialplacestostay.com

Making the most of London

Quick reference indices

including places which are: wheelchair-friendly, good for people of limited mobility, good for walks, good for singles, child-friendly, places with a garden or patio area, places where pets are welcome and places with rooms under £70 a night

What is Alastair Sawday Publishing?

The Little Earth Book – 2nd Edition

Alastair Sawday's Special Places to Stay series

Exchange rate page

Order forms

Report form

Index of Bed & Breakfasts

Index of Hotels

Explanation of symbols

Acknowledgements

Tom Bell wrote this book. He researched it, dreamed of it, cursed and loved it, put it all together and fine-tuned it. He was the only person we thought capable of doing all that with good humour and deep resourcefulness. He had created our hugely successful book on *British Hotels, Inns and Other Places* so brought to bear on London the well-honed tastes and skills of a professional – with the proper enthusiasms of an inspired amateur.

But, perhaps as impressive as Tom's creation of the book was the way he researched it: by bike. Not for him the contour-flattening tube or the breathless crush of the bus. He wheeled freely around the capital on his modern steed, an example to us all. He caused no pollution, no noise – just a touch of angst among motorists, no doubt. Like James Bond, he would slough off his cyclist's garb to slip effortlessly into smooth researcher mode for hotel managers. Those who were unimpressed are, presumably, not in this book.

If you enjoy, with this book, many nights of deep sleep and interesting contacts then you have Tom to thank.

Alastair Sawday

Series editor: .... Alastair Sawday

Editor: .... Tom Bell

Editorial director: .... Annie Shillito

Production manager: .... Julia Richardson

Production assistants: .... Rachel Brook, Tom Dalton

Editorial assistants: .... Jo Boissevain, Laura Kinch

Web editor: .... Russell Wilkinson

Sales & marketing: .... Paula Brown, Sarah Bolton

Accounts: .... Bridget Bishop, Sheila Clifton,
Sandra Hasell, Jenny Purdy

Additional writing: .... Jo Boissevain

Additional photography: .... Quentin Craven

Symbols: .... Mark Brierley

A word from Alastair Sawd.

L ondon – Paris – Prague – what's the difference?! The same heaving crowds of trainer-shod tourists prowl their streets looking for burgers and bargains. The souvenir-stalls and buses clog the streets in the same way. Monstrous multi-nationals jostle each other for space in all three cities. So why come to London if Prague is cheaper and Paris more elegant?

Outrageous! London is the centre of the world, as far as Tom Bell is concerned, and he should know. He has travelled vigorously and widely but lives, loves and breathes the city. His selection of places to stay reflects that passion, for it is eclectic, unusual, inspired and inspiring. From the Dorchester (well-stated elegance) to a barge on the Thames (why not?) and with many fine, family-run B&B's in between, he shares with you the full range of his taste.

There is nothing clichéd about Tom's London, no 'heritage', no banging on familiar drums. There are pubs, open spaces, rides through Richmond Park, walks along the river. With hints from him and advice from the people you will meet through this book, you will catch the vitality and endearing ordinariness of a great, largely civilised, community of souls.

However, a visit to London is too precious to be wasted in a rotten bedroom. For you aren't just sleeping, you are 'feeling' the city, meeting people, learning where to begin, maybe. If you like to meet receptionists at the Hilton and to sleep in a space designed at head office, then this book is not for you. But if you like people, and their different ways of living, then you will enjoy those who run these special places. The exhilarating mix of characters is part of the strength of this book. You can be anonymous, or you can carouse with interesting folk. Just turn these pages and choose.

Please allow me a brief rant: I long for the day when the car no longer dominates our streets and cities – indeed, our lives. Let the citizens of London consider themselves citizens rather than 'motorists'. Then, perhaps, they will dream of a city that uses cars when necessary and otherwise leaves the space between their houses for people, bikes and buses. Other cities have done it. The future, otherwise, is grim: more of the same. Go to Cairo and you will see what lies in store for us. Even better, try biking in London.

This guide is a long-awaited 'first', and if you are just browsing then BUY IT, for you will be ahead of the queue to get into these remarkable places. And do read Tom's Introduction; it is full of fascinating detail and insights.

Alastair Sawday

Introduction

This book assembles a diverse collection of places to stay in London, all providing style, conviviality and value for money. We have excluded places where the smiles are chiselled onto the faces of the staff, and those places that exist solely to part you from your money. We firmly believe that it is not 'what is done' but 'the way things are done' that makes a place special. We remain firmly on the side of the little guy, and we applaud the B&B owners and small hoteliers in this book for their unstinting kindness and generosity.

B&Bs

The B&Bs we feature are smart, lived-in family homes where owners offer a couple of rooms each night for a modest London fee. They are a great rarity in London and hard to unearth; this book is the result of years of research. Do bear in mind when deciding where to stay that these are homes, not hotels: you will often be amazed by the generosity of your hosts, but you will be disappointed if you expect the type of service you would receive in a hotel.

Hotels

The hotels we seek out tend to be smallish and owner-run. We do feature a few small group-owned places and the odd grand place, but no chain hotels; our books are about places that have both style and substance, where the art of hospitality is practised with warmth, good humour and flair.

Space

Space is a rare commodity in central London. Thus, to stay in the middle of town will cost a lot more than to stay a couple of miles out. Most Londoners live away from the centre.

Introduction

Noise

London is a big city with a level of noise that is unavoidable. However, because its residential, retail and business districts tend to stand apart from each other, most residential areas are quiet all day long. Occasionally you get a bit of noise from a pub at closing time, but this is rare. London is quieter at night than you might think. If, however, you are a light sleeper, it is always worth asking for a quiet room when you book.

How to use this book

Bedrooms

We list the different types of rooms available: twins, doubles, twin/doubles (i.e. can be either), singles, triples, family rooms, suites and one or two 'junior suites', a term we prefer to avoid but in these cases it describes a large room with a sitting area. It is always worth checking exactly what's in your room and how big it is; it will help avoid disappointment.

Bathrooms

All rooms have 'en suite' bathrooms unless stated otherwise. Some have en suite showers, some have baths. If you want a particular combination, specify when you book. Very often in B&Bs, private bathrooms are one step outside your bedroom door on a floor that no one else ever uses. We would strongly urge you not to discount rooms simply because they do not have an en suite bathroom.

Price

All prices listed in this book – for hotels and for B&Bs – include VAT (Value Added Tax). The price listed is for two people sharing a room and includes breakfast unless stated otherwise. If no single-occupancy price is listed it means single people pay full whack for a double room. Where a price range is given this may be because rooms are of different sizes or because different rates apply at different times of the week or year. We have made every effort to be accurate, but prices change, usually upwards, so please confirm them when booking. Hotels will often quote prices on the telephone excluding VAT; currently it is 17.5% on top of the purchase price. It is worth knowing that most hotels are busiest on weekdays, so you can often get deals at the weekends. Ring and ask.

estostay.com

Introduction

Meals

A full cooked breakfast is included in the price unless otherwise stated. We also let you know if lunch or dinner are available, and, if so, what the cost is per person. Meals in a B&B are usually served at one table. London is full of great restaurants, so if evening meals are not available you will always find somewhere good and reasonably priced in the neighbourhood. Where I know of good restaurants, I have recommended them in the text, and your hosts will be happy to advise.

Getting about

The nearest tubes, buses or trains are listed. Public transport in London receives much criticism. However, if you do not travel during rush hour (7.30am-9.30am, 4pm-7pm) you will nearly always get a seat on the bus, train or tube.

Buses

Buses are a great way to see London inexpensively and their repeated use is the hallmark of a true Londoner. Bus cards cost £2 a day and allow unlimited travel; you can buy them at most newsagent's. Buses are slower than tubes but you get to see London. The letter 'N' before a bus number denotes a night bus; many of London's buses are 24-hour. The web site www.transportforlondon.gov.uk/buses is excellent, interactive, and has information on every bus route in Greater London. Otherwise, **London Travel Information** (020 7222 1234) will help.

The tube

The tube is the most popular way to get around town, but it can be expensive with a one-way ticket from zone 1 to zone 2 costing a crazy £1.90. Travel cards cost £4.10 a day (zones 1 and 2), but you can't use them until after 9.30am. They are valid for buses as well. Weekend travel cards cost £6 (zones 1 and 2). Londoners use weekly travel cards (£19, zones 1 and 2). They give total access to buses and tubes, 24 hours a day, but you'll need a passport photo when you buy the card. You can get to Heathrow on the Piccadilly line and to City Airport via the Docklands Light Railway, a new line that heads east, and south, from Bank and Tower Hill tube stations respectively: see www.dlr.co.uk. There is a tube map at the front of this book. **London Travel Information** (020 7222 1234) can answer most questions. Also see www.thetube.com.

Trains

Local trains into London's big stations are often the quickest way in and out of town. For example, the fast train from Richmond to Waterloo

Introduction

(eight trains an hour) takes 12 minutes; you can do Crystal Palace to Victoria in 20 minutes. Your hosts should have timetables. Airport trains are useful, too. The **Heathrow Express** (0845 600 1515) from Paddington Station costs £12 one way, £22 return, leaves every 15 minutes (5am-midnight), and takes 20 minutes (the tube to Heathrow is about a quarter the price, but takes longer). The **Gatwick Express** (08705 301530) from Victoria Station costs £10.50 single, £20 return, leaves every 15 minutes between 5.50am and midnight (then hourly until 5.20am) and takes about 35 minutes. The **Stansted Express** (08705 301530) from Liverpool Street Station costs £12 one way, £22 return, leaves every 15-30 minutes depending on when you travel and takes about 45 minutes. It's quicker than a taxi. As is **Eurostar** (08705 186 186), which will whisk you off to Paris in three hours (15+ trains a day) or Brussels in two and a half (ten a day). It leaves from Waterloo Station. Book 14 days in advance, stay either a Saturday night or two week nights, and the price is £79 return. Eurostar often has 'specials', so ring to find out. **National Rail Enquiries** (08457 484950) will tell you the time of any train in Britain. Also see www.thetrainline.com.

Walking

In central London walking is the best way to get around. You can cut through parks and back streets and step off the tourist trail. Buy the *A-Z*, the London street guide, available just about anywhere; you won't get lost if you do. Various walking tours exist and are usually well-priced at about £5. Try **Original London Walks** (020 7624 3978 or www.walks.com). **Open House Architecture** (020 7267 644 or www.londonopenhouse.org) is more expensive (£18.50), but worth the price. They take you round London's great buildings, both old and new, and spill the historical beans as they do. There are many guides detailing London walks and you can buy them in most London bookshops.

Cycling

This is the quickest way to get around town, but London's streets are packed and you should expect no courtesy from drivers. You can rent mountain bikes or hybrids at the following places: **Bikepark** (020 7731 7012) at 63 New King's Road, SW6: £12 first day, £6 second, £4 third,

Introduction

£200 credit card deposit, or **London Bicycle Tour Company** (020 7928 6838) at 1a Gabriel's Wharf, 56 Upper Ground, SE1: £12 first day, £6 second, £36 a week, credit card deposit required; they also lead bike tours and you can hire roller blades, too. If the idea of cycling around London is too scary for you, try the **Original Bicycle Hire Company** (0800 013 8000), Roehampton Gate, Richmond Park. You can hire bikes by the day or half-day in summer and there's a beautiful perimeter track around the park (8 miles). It's a fantastic day out, very popular, and Richmond Park is easily London's most beautiful. There are food and drink stalls along the route or you can bring a picnic.

Taxis and mini cabs
Taxis are expensive and their prices rise still further after 10pm, though you should try a black cab once. Drivers are all licensed and you can hail them on the street. Mini cabs – ordinary cars – are less expensive, but not as stylish, and you have to ring for them. Never pick one up on the streets; it is illegal and drivers are not registered. **Addison Lee** is a reliable firm and covers the whole of London (020 7387 8888). **Lady Cabs** (020 7254 3501) has female drivers only. Always ask the price when you're on the phone.

Boats
Boats from Westminster Pier to Greenwich run all year round and cost £6 one way, £7.50 return. The trip takes about an hour. Westminster to Hampton Court (via Richmond and Kew Gardens) runs April to October and costs £10 one way, £14 return. The trip takes three hours one way, so travel there or back by train (Hampton Court station). Trains go to/from Waterloo, via Clapham Junction or Vauxhall and take 30 minutes. Both trips are well worth the time and money. There are other boats operating on the Thames. Most leave from Westminster Pier, The Embankment, SW1 (Westminster tube). **London Travel Information** (020 7222 1234) offers timetables and advice, or see www.transportforlondon.gov.uk/river.

Introduction

Parking

We list the cost if there is one, and the type of parking space – either
on-street, off-street or in a car park. It may be that you can park free on
the street at night but that during the day there is a 2 hour maximum stay.
If you want to park in central London, it'll cost you a fortune (about
£25 a day in a car park). If you want to park a few miles out, it's cheaper
(about £10 a day, on-street). If you want to park about five miles out,
it's free (and often off-street in your host's drive). If you must drive to
London, the last thing you'll want to do while you're here is to drive in it.
The streets are clogged with traffic; they'll drive you crazy.

Deposits

You should expect to book your accommodation in advance, and even
to pay a deposit. If you cancel you should expect to lose the deposit –
or, at least, some of it – unless your room is re-let, in which case you may
expect to have it refunded in full. Check the exact terms when booking
and ask the B&B or hotel to confirm the agreement in writing.

Problems, problems

If you have a problem, however trivial, do tell your host or owner or
manager about it; they are primed, one hopes, to solve it at a stroke.
Owners always say "if only I'd known" when we contact them after the
event. Do give them that chance. But if you get nowhere, or if you are
met with downright rudeness, please let us know.

Tipping

Tipping is normal only in restaurants in Britain, though you may wish
to reward exceptional service or kindness.

Telephones

The per-unit cost of telephoning from hotels is exorbitant. Check the
per-minute cost before making a call. Hotels often give vague figures, but
manage to be extremely precise on your bill. Insist on knowing exactly how
much they will charge you (probably £1 a minute, local) before you call.
The code for America from England is 011.

Laundry

Most places will do laundry for you. The hotels do this as a matter of
course, but if you ask a B&B owner they will nearly always help (especially
if you are staying for three or four nights), or let you do it yourself.
A small fee will usually be charged.

Introduction

Credit cards

In hotels, Visa and MasterCard are invariably accepted, American Express is sometimes welcome, Diners Club hardly ever. B&Bs, however, rarely accept credit cards so pay by cash or British cheque.

Smoking

A symbol tells you if a place is totally non-smoking. Most B&Bs are; most hotels aren't. B&B owners will often give you an ashtray (and an umbrella) and let you explore their garden if you so wish! Hotels have smoking areas but bedrooms and dining rooms are usually smoke-free zones.

Children

Child-friendly B&Bs may not have all the kit that a child-friendly hotel would have. Please don't assume there will be cots etc. In the hotels, baby-listening and baby-sitting services are often available.

Booking agencies

Some of the B&Bs listed in this book use an agency to take their bookings.

Subscriptions

All the places in this book have paid a small fee to be included in it. It helps with the high production costs that come with an all-colour book. But this is a fee, not a bribe! People absolutely cannot buy their way in.

Introduction

Disclaimer

We make no claims to pure objectivity in judging our special places to stay. They are here because we like them. Our opinions and tastes are ours alone and this book is a statement of them; we hope you will share them. We have done our utmost to get our facts right but apologise for any mistakes that may have crept in. Sometimes, too, prices shift, usually upwards, and 'things' change. We should be grateful to be told of any errors and changes.

The environment

We try to reduce our impact on the environment where possible by:

- planting trees to compensate for our carbon emissions (as calculated by Edinburgh University): we are officially a Carbon Neutral® publishing company. The emissions directly related with the paper production, printing and distribution of this book have been made Carbon Neutral® through the planting of indigenous woodlands with Future Forests

- re-using paper, recycling stationery, tins, bottles, etc.

- encouraging staff use of bicycles (they're loaned free) and car sharing

- celebrating the use of organic, home – and locally-produced food

- publishing books that support, in however small a way, the rural economy and small-scale businesses

- encouraging our owners to follow recommendations made by the Energy Efficiency Centre to make their homes more environmentally friendly

www.specialplacestostay.com

Our web site has online entries for many of the places featured here and in our other books, with up-to-date information and direct links to their own e-mail addresses and web sites. You'll find more about the site at the back of this book.

And finally

Do let us know how you got on in these places, and if you know and love a place that we have not included. There is a report form at the back of the book or you can e-mail london@sawdays.co.uk. If your recommendation leads to a place being included in a future edition, you'll receive a free guide.

Tom Bell

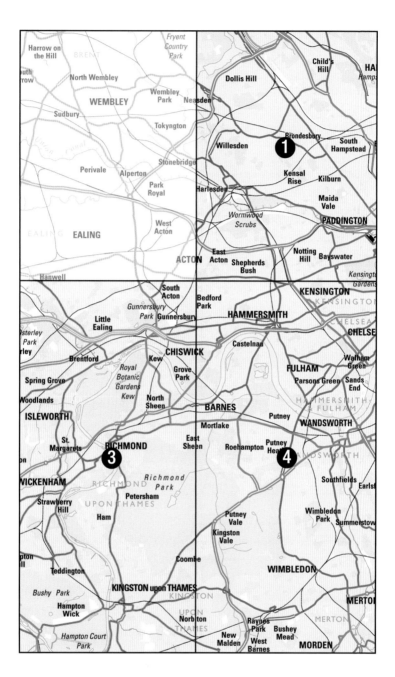

A guide to our map page numbers

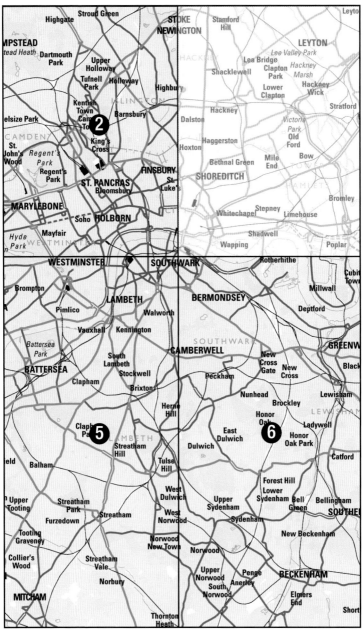

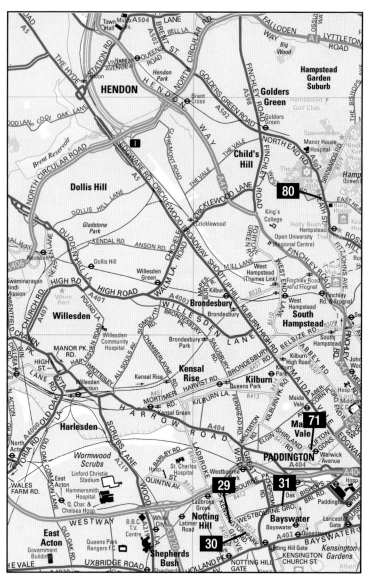

Map 1

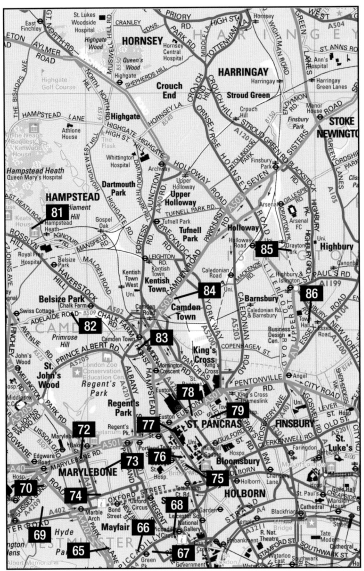

Map 2

© Bartholomew Ltd 2002

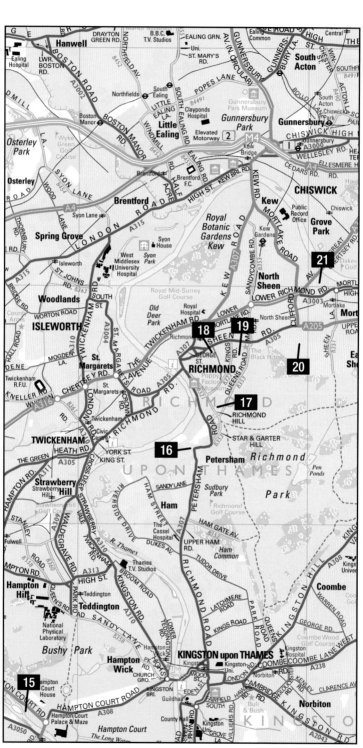

Map 3

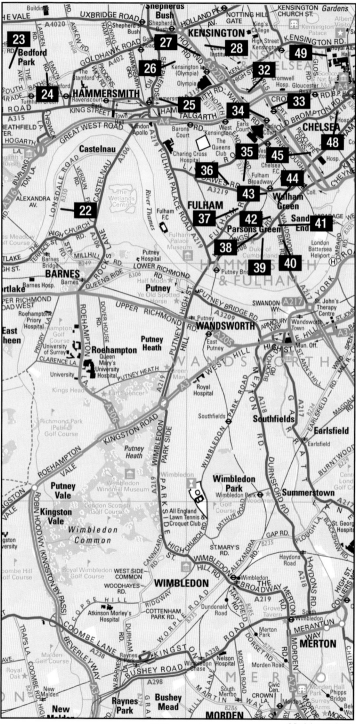

Map 4

© Bartholomew Ltd 2002

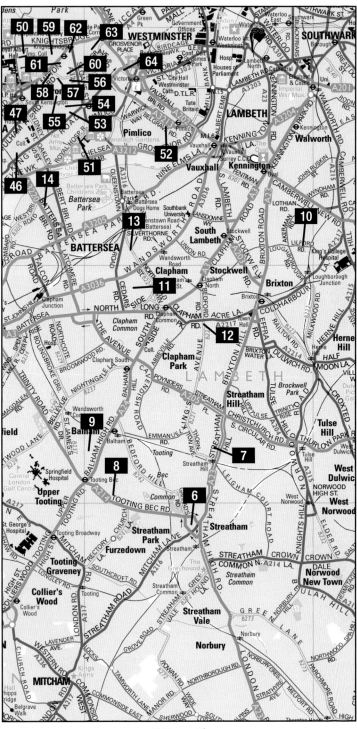

Map 5

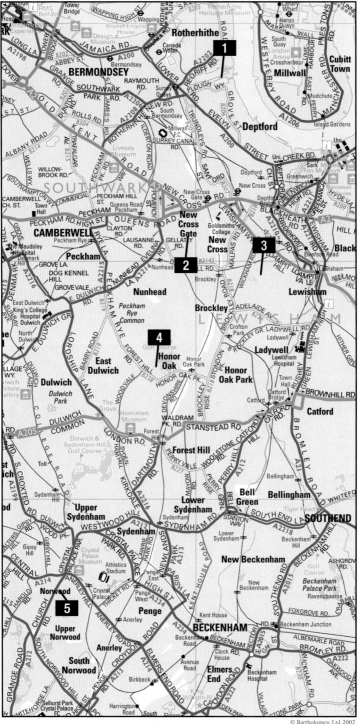

Map 6

© Bartholomew Ltd 2002

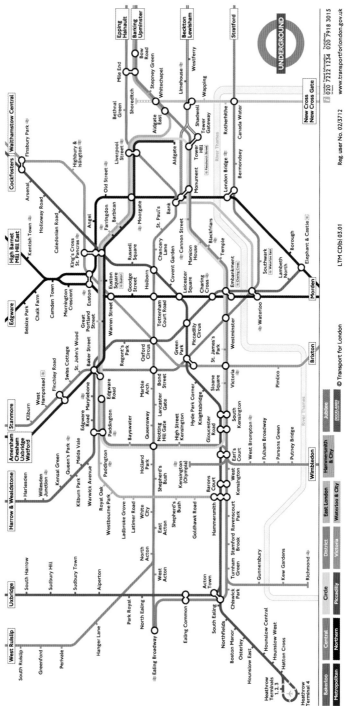

South of the River

Henley-on-Thames
New Cross Gate, Brockley
East Dulwich
Crystal Palace
Streatham, Balham
Camberwell
Clapham Common
Battersea

Battersea Power Station

I thought of London spread out in the sun,
Its postal districts packed like squares of wheat.
Philip Larkin, 'The Whitsun Weddings'

Rival

PO Box 4553	**Tel:** 07976 390 416
Henley-on-Thames	**E-mail:** rivalbarge@orange.net
Oxfordshire RG9 3XZ	**Web:** www.rivalbarge.com

Michael Clayton-Smith & Frances Northcott

This one's a bit complicated – a tale of two seasons. 'Rival', a 1925 Luxmotor barge, spent her working life on Dutch canals, but in retirement crossed the channel and fell into Michael's hands. He gave her a make-over, top to toe. She now shines: varnished mahogany interiors, the original wheel in the wheelhouse, a woodburner in the saloon, even heated towel rails in compact shower rooms (Michael was once a plumber). A real sense of adventure: the high seas close to the high street – well, almost. 'Rival' is moored in London from October to March at South Dock, Canada Water (though this may change to St Katharine's Dock at Tower Bridge, or to Chiswick), and you can stay for B&B during these months. In summer, she heads to Henley and messes about on the river. Here you can B&B, or cruise from Hampton Court to Henley via Windsor. Breakfast on deck, stop at pubs for lunch, see the sights, walk the Thames path – whatever you like – then seek refuge on board at night. As for Frances, she was senior British springboard diving champion at the age of 12 and went to the Tokyo Olympics; like 'Rival', incredible.

Rooms: 3: 2 double cabins and 1 twin cabin. For group cruises a further cabin and double sofabed are available.
Price: B&B: £75-£95; singles from £60. Group cruises from £67 per person per day for B&B; half- and full-board cruises are also available.
Meals: Full breakfast included.
Closed: Occasionally.

Tube: Surrey Quays; Canada Water.
Bus: 47, 188.
Parking: Free on-street.

Map: 6

113 Pepys Road

New Cross Gate
London SE14 5SE

Tel: 020 7639 1060
Fax: 020 7639 8780
E-mail: annemarten@pepysroad.com
Web: www.pepysroad.com

Anne & Tim Marten

Anne is originally from Borneo, Tim was 'our man in East Malaysia' 35 years ago. They have travelled widely, are full of life, and now live on the side of a hill above a carpet of London lights. Hats on the hat stand, old maps on the walls. Anne has spared no expense in the decoration of her home and it sparkles as a result. The downstairs room is worthy of an expensive hotel, a room where east meets west. The plushest of carpets, the biggest of beds, the crispest linen, then bamboo blinds, Chinese screens, porcelain lamps and lacquered panels. There are kimonos in the wardrobe, scrolls on the walls and a bathroom of marble, mirror and Chinese porcelain; it shines so brightly it may dazzle you. Upstairs, two more bedrooms, one in country house style, the other more contemporary in yellow; both are lovely, the top-floor bathroom a delight. Anne cooks brilliantly and will do you a steaming hot oriental cooked breakfast or the 'full English'. If you eat in at night, you might get smoked salmon, roast grouse and chocolate pudding. It's a short walk downhill to New Cross Gate for bus, tube and train. Wonderful.

Rooms: 3: 1 double and 1 twin/double; 1 twin, private bathroom.
Price: £75-£85; singles from £37.50.
Meals: Full breakfast included (oriental breakfast by arrangement). Dinner, by arrangement, £26 (BYO wine).
Closed: Occasionally.

Train: New Cross Gate (to London Bridge).
Tube: New Cross, New Cross Gate.
Bus: 21, 36, 53, 171, 172.
Parking: Free on-street.

Map: 6

2

57 Breakspears Road

Brockley
London SE4 1XR

Tel: 020 8469 3162
Fax: 020 8469 3162
E-mail: bunzl@btinternet.com

Biddy Bunzl

Not a hard house to find – just knock at the door of the wildest pad on the street. Biddy paints professionally and her work – abstract modern, splashy colours – hangs everywhere. Her 1860s home is an extension of both work and self: funky, easy-going and downright welcoming. I arrived at lunchtime and was plied with delicious pumpkin soup, goats' cheese and fresh bread. The house has big, light-swamped rooms, high ceilings, polished wood floors and groovy colours everywhere – 21st-century B&B. The hub is the big kitchen in red and yellow with its farmhouse table for generous breakfasts, but most dazzling among the many jewels of Number 57 is the garden onto which the kitchen's wall of glass opens. Biddy's other half, James, is a Kiwi garden designer – one of London's best – and if you're after a bit of subtropical forest in South London, then this is the place to find it. Wander at will and find old dock timbers, a water garden, a sari-shaded Mexican hammock, Manuka poles and various grasses, some five feet tall. Tea-dances down the road at the Rivoli Ballroom, an architectural gem, are meant to be a lot of fun! Fantastic.

Rooms: 1 twin.
Price: £70-£80; singles £45.
Meals: Full breakfast included.
Closed: Never.

Train: Brockley (to London Bridge).
Bus: 36, 171, 172.
Parking: Free on-street.

Map: 6

Shepherd's

39 Marmora Road
East Dulwich
London SE22 0RX

Tel: 020 8693 4355
Fax: 020 8693 7954
Web: www.shepherdslondon.com

Brian & Penny Shepherd

A quirky little place, about a mile from the unmissable Dulwich Picture Gallery, which dates back to the 1790s and was set up by the King of Poland (the gallery, that is). A sinful place, too, at least the biscuits were: home-made by Brian and irresistible. Bedrooms here will have you writing home – plates of fruit with napkins and knives, Indian wall hangings, gold silky bedspreads, colourful window boxes, wooden beds, rag-rolled walls, bold colours, rugs on stripped floors... and packs of playing cards. Brian will chauffeur you around London (or Britain) in his 1954 Inspector-Maigret-style Citröen: leather seats, wooden dash, running boards. A glass of wine or beer on arrival, a lovely big open-plan kitchen/dining room ("guests can see if we burn their breakfast"), and a different cooked dish every morning. Dinners, too: fish soup, rack of lamb, chocolate pud. Not a place for weight-watchers, but, if you are one, Brian and Penny will probably devise something brilliant for you. There's a grand piano which you're welcome to play, two dogs, one cat and views over London. Station pick-ups and drop-offs, too.

Rooms: 5: 1 double; 1 double and 1 twin, both private bathroom; 1 double and 1 single sharing bathroom.
Price: £70-£80 (2-night minimum); singles from £45.
Meals: Full breakfast incl. Dinner, by arrangement, £25 incl. wine. Room service.
Closed: Never.
Train: Honour Oak Park (to London Bridge and Victoria); West Dulwich (to Victoria).
Bus: 12, 63.
Parking: Free on-street.

Map: 6

4

24 Fox Hill

Crystal Palace
London SE19 2XE

Tel: 020 8768 0059
Fax: 020 8768 0063
E-mail: suehaigh@foxhill-bandb.co.uk
Web: www.foxhill-bandb.co.uk

Sue & Tim Haigh

Wander around at the top of the hill for views over London... about 30 miles of them. Sue and Tim have renovated with style. They moved out of central London for the space, the trees, the sky... all of which you get in abundance. Shades of the Raj as you enter, with old pictures of stern gentlemen in pith helmets (one of them Sue's grandfather). Then come the wall-hangings, some Sue's work – she is a recent graduate of Chelsea Art College and has a studio at the back. Inside: wooden floors, warm rugs, a Swedish stove in the sitting room, and a wall of books on the landing. Beautiful bedrooms are full of antiques and paintings; the biggest has a sofa and candelabra. At breakfast, sit at the kitchen table and look out onto the tree that Pissarro painted in 1870; then hop on a train and go see the painting – it hangs in the National Gallery. When you return, Sue will cook supper (sea bass, maybe, stuffed with herbs). Or dine out nearby; you can eat your way around the world (even eel pie and mash). There's a fantastic bookshop at the top of the hill and don't forget your walk in the park. Oh, and their lovely garden, too.

Rooms: 3: 1 twin/double;
1 twin and 1 single sharing shower.
Price: £80-£100; singles from £40.
Meals: Full breakfast included.
Dinner, by arrangement, £25-£30.
Closed: Never.

Train: Crystal Palace
(to Victoria or London Bridge).
Bus: 2, 3.
Parking: Free on-street.

Map: 6

34 Ambleside Avenue

Streatham
London SW16 1QP

Tel: 020 8769 2742
Fax: 020 8677 3023
E-mail: info@bednbrek.com
Web: www.bednbrek.com

Chris & Viveka Collingwood

A beautiful pyracantha tree guards the front of this handsome 1880s red-brick house. There's history, too; Emily Pankhurst held meetings here, and the house once belonged to Carl Davis, the American film composer. Chris and Viveka give generously of their space and time. There's a snug library-sitting room with fenders round the fire and a stylish dining room flanked by tromp l'oeil pillars. This is a smart family home, with bedrooms that fit the bill: comfy beds, mahogany furniture, pretty fabrics, tartan blankets and, in one room, photos of a trip to the Hindu Kush. Best of all is the huge room at the top. It has two sofas, yet there's enough room for a game of football. It also has twin beds hidden up in the eaves, so it's perfect for families. Viveka does a continental breakfast, but you can go Swedish and have jam on your cheese, if you like; there's a pretty walled garden where you can polish it off in good weather. Chris will pick you up from the station, drop you off at the tube. He also knows his Streatham history. Famous sons include David Garrick, Edmund Burke, Joshua Reynolds and Dr Johnson.

Rooms: 3: 1 double and 1 twin sharing bathroom and shower; 1 family room for 4, private shower.
Price: £60-£70; singles from £45.
Meals: Continental breakfast included.
Closed: Occasionally.

Train: Streatham Hill or Streatham Common (to Victoria).
Tube: Tooting Bec.
Bus: 133, 159, 319.
Parking: Free off-street.

Map: 5

38 Killieser Avenue

Streatham
London SW2 4NT

Tel: 020 8671 4196
Fax: 020 8671 4196
E-mail: winklehaworth@hotmail.com

Winkle & Philip Haworth

If, for even a moment, you think this Streatham dream isn't worth the bother, come and prove yourself wrong. Few people do things with as much natural good humour and style as Winkle. The Haworths – early Streatham pioneers – have brought country-house chic to South London. The house glows 'mellow yellow.' You breakfast in the rug-strewn, wooden-floored, farmhouse kitchen, but can decamp in spring or summer to the spectacular garden: agapanthus, pink wisteria, roses by the dozen, tulips and jasmine – 20 years of dedicated hard work, a splendid spot for bacon and eggs. At the front door, umbrellas, tennis rackets and a grandfather clock. Upstairs, big bedrooms are grand and homely: more rugs, comfy beds, lamb's wool blankets, loads of books, waffle bathrobes, beautiful linen: Winkle does nothing by halves. There's a generous single, with a writing desk, a large armchair and views onto this quiet residential street. Streatham Hill station is a three-minute walk; you can be in Victoria in 15 minutes, but even if it took an hour, it'd be worth the trouble. Brilliant.

Rooms: 2: 1 twin and 1 single sharing bathroom.
Price: £80-£90; singles £50-£60.
Meals: Full breakfast included. Dinner, by arrangement, £25.
Closed: Occasionally.

Train: Streatham Hill (to Victoria).
Tube: Balham (15-minute walk).
Bus: 137, 159, 319.
Parking: Free off-street.

108 Streathbourne Road

Balham
London SW17 8QY

Tel: 020 8767 6931
Fax: 020 8672 8839
E-mail: mary.hodges@virgin.net

Mary & David Hodges

This is an Aussie-English partnership, Mary being a Sydneysider who has infiltrated Parliament – she works for an MP, so tours can easily be arranged. Their 1880 terraced home is in a quiet tree-lined street, part of a conservation area. Tooting Common is at the end of the road (thus soundproofing further), and its lido – something of a South London institution – is supposedly the largest in the world (or coldest?). Exercise freaks can head off pre-breakfast, do their lengths, then return to find a fire in the dining room and defrost. You get the newspaper, too, and croissants, and if the weather's good, doors open up to a pretty London garden. Pots of geraniums sit on the window ledge outside the bedroom; inside you find an armchair, a writing desk and a big comfy walnut bed. Sheets and blankets or duvets – whatever you want; a very pretty room. In the hall on the wall a great aunt... well, her portrait anyway. There's a twin room upstairs, so you can bring the children. Even better, they can bring you. Finally, if you eat here in the evenings, David, who works in wine, puts a bottle on the table.

Rooms: 2: 1 double with bathroom;
1 twin with private bathroom
(same-party bookings only).
Price: £60-£70; singles from £30.
Meals: Continental breakfast included.
Dinner, by arrangement, £20.
Closed: Occasionally.

Train: Balham (to Victoria).
Tube: Tooting Bec.
Bus: 155, 319.
Parking: £2.50 a day on-street,
free at weekends.

Map: 5

The Coach House

2 Tunley Road
Balham
London SW17 7QJ

Tel: 020 8772 1939
Fax: 0870 133 4957
E-mail: coachhouse@chslondon.com
Web: www.coachhouse.chslondon.com

Meena & Harley Nott

This was home to the man who built the street and he built himself a coach house, too... for which you will thank him as it is now a very pretty studio at the back of the house. Meena and Harley came here two years ago and have renovated completely, with Meena, an interior designer, making sure that both inside and outside scrubbed up brilliantly. In the main house, shiny wooden floors, loads of rugs and the odd exotic touch, be it a (fake) zebra-skinned chair or a three-foot-high vase on a four-foot-high plinth. Here you eat: breakfast, a one-hour feast (anything from porridge to poached eggs) and, if you want, a five course evening meal, organic, which starts with "the ceremony of the sherry" before "starter, soup, fish, meat, cheese and fruit," so don't expect to go hungry. Across the terracotta-potted courtyard you come to the coach house, decorated in country style. The room under the eaves is open to the rafters, French windows open to flowers, and there are *toile de Jouy* fabrics, rugs on wooden floors and masses of space. It's all yours, and it's very pretty, very quiet and close to the tube. Perfect.

Rooms: 2: 1 double/family;
1 twin with private shower
(same-party bookings only).
Price: £75-£110 for two people;
£85-£125 for three;
£130-£175 for up to five.
Meals: Full breakfast included. Dinner,
by arrangement (5 courses), £30-£40.
Closed: Never.
Train: Balham (to Victoria).
Tube: Balham.
Bus: 155, 319.
Parking: £5 a day on-street.

119 Knatchbull Road

Camberwell
London SE5 9QY

Tel: 020 7738 7878
Fax: 020 7738 6788
E-mail: jackrockuk@aol.com

Jackie Rokotnitz

These huge houses were built by a wealthy Huguenot in the 1860s – his 'grand gesture'; this one was originally Number Nine! Jackie's home is big and bright: huge rooms, high ceilings, a wonderful sweeping cast-iron staircase, and the sort of space you rarely find in London. One of the bedrooms on the top floor has its own open fire, as does the breakfast room, so you can toast yourself – and your bread – on winter mornings. Jackie renovates houses, so expect some style, though it's not a fussy place. Go for the rooms at the top if you can; they are massive and delightfully furnished with country quilts, big porcelain lamps, sofas and armchairs, carafes of water, lots of good wooden furniture and plenty to read. The odd piece of wild art hangs on the wall (Jackie's son is an artist), and there's a small swimming pool down in the basement where you swim against the waves. Don't miss Camberwell, its markets, arts' week (June) and restaurants. Myatts Fields, just down the road, is an exquisite and well-preserved London garden, with bandstand et al; you'll be missing out if you don't see it.

Rooms: 4: 2 doubles;
1 twin and 1 single sharing shower
(same-party bookings only).
Price: £65-£75; singles £35.
Meals: Help-yourself continental breakfast
included.
Closed: Occasionally.

Train: Brixton (10-minute walk).
Tube: Brixton (10-minute walk).
Bus: 3, 36, 159, 185.
Parking: Free on-street.

Map: 5

8 Macaulay Road

Clapham Common
London SW4 0QX

Tel: 020 7622 9603
Fax: 020 7720 8094
E-mail: susiepriestley@aol.com

Susie & Jeremy Priestley

Clapham, with its sea of green common lapping at its pavements, is a place to come and see the sky – not an easy task in London. It has a village feel and fiercely loyal residents, but the secret's out and transmigrating Londoners now come to sample the delicacies of its bars and restaurants. The houses of Macaulay Road were built for prosperous Victorian merchants: big rooms, high ceilings, large gardens, all of which survive at Susie's warm and welcoming family home. The nerve centre here is the wonderful flowered conservatory/dining room which looks onto a balustraded terrace and a cool, green, tree-shaded lawn. Delicious breakfasts are taken in peace and quiet with the newspaper. The house is immaculate throughout: stained glass in the front door, limestone tiles in the hall, polished brass stair rods, and cricket bats in the kitchen (the Priestleys have three teenage sons). Bright and airy bedrooms in country-house style are huge, with fine linen, fresh flowers and Robert's radios. A great place to stay, with the tube close by, the best bus in London (the 137), and the common on your doorstep.

Rooms: 3: 1 twin/double, 1 single, both with private bathrooms; 1 occasional double.
Price: £96-£105; singles from £40.
Meals: Full breakfast included.
Closed: Occasionally.

Tube: Clapham Common.
Bus: 88, 137.
Parking: Free off-street.

Map: 5

22 Northbourne Road

Clapham Common
London SW4 7DT

Tel: 020 7720 4871
Fax: 020 7622 6803
E-mail: cliveder@tinyworld.co.uk

Libby & Clive de Rougemont

Another row of beautiful Clapham houses, this one mid-1800s and close to both tube and common. Smart black railings on guard at the front, then steps up to the front door. This is a large family house spread over four floors. The dining room on the lower ground has a smart red carpet and big mahogany table, and there's a 160-foot garden out back, patrolled, occasionally, by two (lazy) border terriers. Up a floor to a very English drawing room: high ceilings, marble fireplace, family portraits and some lovely pieces. Your ascent up to the bedrooms is likely to pass the odd ski suit (Libby sells them) and is rewarded by a large room with garden views. Expect fresh flowers, good fabrics, bowls of fruit, a pretty dressing table, lots of books and lots of space. There's a bathroom across the way. The restaurants of Clapham wait: try Maharani's curry house or Eco for pizza (very popular, so book ahead). If you want to take the bus into town, the 88 passes Tate Britain, the Houses of Parliament, Downing Street and Trafalgar Square.

Rooms: 1 twin/double, private bathroom.
Price: £70-£80; singles from £60.
Meals: Full breakfast included.
Closed: Occasionally.

Tube: Clapham Common.
Bus: 88, 137, 345.
Parking: Free on-street.

Map: 5

20 St Philip Street

Battersea
London SW8 3SL

Tel: 020 7498 9967
Fax: 020 7498 9967
E-mail: barbaragraham@telco4u.net

Barbara Graham

A delightful, double-fronted, terraced cottage, built in 1890 by the Peabody Trust. Barbara loves having guests and is extremely generous, pretty much giving you the run of the house. You breakfast in the dining room by the original Victorian fireplace – the full English works, of course. Across the hall in the sitting room there's a piano; you are welcome to play… or cajole Barbara into a tune. She was an orchestral musician (oboe) and I bet she's better than she says she is. The lovely sitting room has gilt-framed mirrors, wooden blinds, a plump-cushioned sofa, while out back, a small courtyard garden bursts with summer colour. Upstairs, a very comfy bedroom with padded headboard, thick curtains, pretty linen, books, guides, mirrors – nothing has been overlooked. The next-door bathroom is fabulous with porthole windows, a huge mirror and a radio to entertain you as you soak. As for things to do: Battersea Park is lovely; if you stay during the Chelsea Flower Show, you can walk through it on your way. Cirque du Soleil – the French-Canadian circus troupe – have their London home at Battersea Power Station.

Rooms: 1 double, private bathroom.
Price: £80; singles £60.
Meals: Full breakfast included.
Closed: Occasionally.

Train: Queenstown Road (to Waterloo); Battersea Park (to Victoria).
Bus: 137 (to Sloane Square tube).
Parking: £4 a day on-street Monday-Friday.

Map: 5

Worfield Street

Battersea
London SW11 4RB

Tel: 020 7223 1243
E-mail: michael_bradley@ukgateway.net

Catriona & Michael Bradley

A skip and a jump over Albert Bridge (the pretty one with the lights which appears in all the films) and you are in deepest Chelsea and the pleasure dome of the King's Road. On your doorstep is Battersea Park, with lake, zoo, bandstand, pagoda and a tremendous firework display each November 5th. Catriona's 1880 Victorian terraced house is a great find: very pretty and excellent value for money. You get the room at the top, a huge room under the eaves, with sky lights on each side. It is bright, light and colourful, with masses of space. There's lots of art about the house, and you get drapes on your ceiling, the odd modern oil, sparkling cushions on the sofa (it turns into a bed and can easily cope with a couple of small children) and a huge rubber tree bursting from one corner. Breakfast is a movable feast: you can either have it in bed or down in the kitchen. Catriona will also cook you supper, if you want – maybe spaghetti bolognese or roast chicken. Alternatively, there are lots of local restaurants: the Duke of Cambridge is excellent, especially its Sunday lunch. There's jazz in the park in summer, too.

Rooms: 1 double (and 1 double sofabed) with private shower.
Price: £65-£75; singles from £45.
Meals: Continental breakfast included.
Closed: Occasionally.

Tube: South Kensington; Sloane Square (both a 20-minute walk).
Bus: 19, 49, 319, 345.
Parking: £5 a day on-street.

West, South West

Hampton Court
Richmond
Mortlake
Barnes
Bedford Park
Stamford Brook

Battersea Park

Go down to Kew in lilac-time, in lilac-time, in lilac-time
Go down to Kew in lilac-time (it isn't far from London!)

Alfred Noyes, 'The Barrel-Organ'

Paddock Lodge

The Green
Hampton Court
KT8 9BW

Tel: 020 8979 5254
E-mail: 101723.1100@compuserve.com

Dr Louis & Sonia Marks

Two acres of garden include rose, secret, sunken, walled and vegetable, and 100 yards of river frontage, so come by boat if you have one. From the front door you can see the Royal Mews of Hampton Court Palace, which is spectacular. The palace itself is a five-minute walk, one of London's 'ummissables', home of Henry VIII and a favourite royal residence until George II; polish off one of Sonia's delicious breakfasts, then wander over for the day. Return to a gorgeous Georgian/Edwardian house of high arched windows and ornate moulded ceilings. The main bedroom is huge, decorated beautifully in blues and whites, with river views, antique furniture and a panelled bathroom. The smaller bedroom has a brass bed and views of the Royal Mews. Tea and home-baked cakes every day, and Sonia will cook you dinner if you like, much of it home-grown. Hire bikes and follow the Thames, or drive to Kew, Windsor or Wisley. Hampton Court holds various festivals – music, flower, needlework – throughout the year. Fabulous.

Rooms: 2: 2 doubles,
1 with private bathroom.
Price: £88-£98; singles from £55.
Meals: Full breakfast included.
Dinner, 3 courses, £25, by arrangement.
Closed: Occasionally.

Train: Hampton Court (to Waterloo).
Parking: Free off-street.

Map: 3

15

147 Petersham Road

Richmond
TW10 7AH

Tel: 020 8940 3424
E-mail: sylviapeile@peile.force9.co.uk

Sylvia & Robin Peile

A stunning home, originally built in 1700, with exquisite brickwork at the front. Sylvia couldn't be nicer, nor her family for that matter, and Emily, her daughter, obligingly took me on a tour while Sylvia finished up with the curtain lady. "We're not professional," said Sylvia when we sat down for coffee (perhaps not knowing she couldn't have said a better thing), though she was being a little economical with the truth, especially given the fact that breakfast is served in a room that would fit well into a small French château. Oils on the walls, antiques jostling for attention, rugs on ancient wooden floors – a splendid spot for bacon and eggs. The bedroom is at the back of the house; my notes read, "shining white, mahogany dresser, lovely fabrics, total peace." It also has a delightful bathroom. The house is a couple of miles outside Richmond, 200 yards from an entrance to the park, where you can ride, hire bikes, walk or picnic. Turn left out of the drive and at the end of the lane you come to the Thames; you can walk beside it into town, past fields of grazing cattle. The Great River Race passes by in September. Superb.

Rooms: 1 twin, private bathroom.
Price: £60-£70; singles £30-£35.
Meals: Full breakfast included.
Closed: Occasionally.

Train: Richmond (to Waterloo).
Tube: Richmond.
Bus: 65, 371.
Parking: Free off-street.

Map: 3

Doughty Cottage

142A Richmond Hill
Richmond
TW10 6RN

Tel: 020 8332 9434
Fax: 020 8948 3716
E-mail: mail@doughtycottage.com
Web: www.doughtycottage.com

Denise & Samantha O'Neill

Everything here is special: the view at the front, tumbling downhill to a meandering river Thames; the secret garden through which you enter; the house itself – a beautiful 1750s Regency cottage that once belonged to Sir Francis Cooke – and the bedrooms, flamboyantly designed with rich colours and in impeccable style. There are murals in bathrooms, and four-poster beds. The two downstairs rooms have their own private gardens, where, surrounded by terracotta pots, urns, statues and the sweet smell of jasmine, you can breakfast in summer. All this is the work of Denise and Samantha, a mother-and-daughter team who also have a home in Portugal and do alternate months in each (so don't feel too sorry for them). Walk about the place and pass busts, candles, a rocking horse... and enchanted guests. And I'm sure I saw an angel somewhere. There are oils, thick fabrics, Italian beds. The room at the top is huge, with ceilings open to the rafters and river views – a honeymooners' paradise. Fabulous bathrooms, sparkling clean, big fluffy towels, the works. Richmond Park is a two-minute walk away.

Rooms: 3: 1 double; 1 twin/double;
1 double, private bathroom.
Price: Price: £75-£110; singles from £70.
Meals: Continental breakfast included.
Closed: Occasionally.

Train: Richmond (to Waterloo).
Tube: Richmond.
Bus: 65, 371.
Parking: Free off-street.

Map: 3

Chalon House

8 Spring Terrace
Paradise Road
Richmond
TW9 1LW

Tel: 020 8332 1121
Fax: 020 8332 1131
E-mail: virgilioz@aol.com

Ann & Virgilio Zaina

A 1740s house in the heart of Richmond from which you can strike out and wander old alleyways, watch cricket on the green or walk along the towpath by the river. Ann gets lots of Londoners who want to escape the city at weekends, though the registry office is just around the corner, so come to get married instead. She also does things impeccably: convivial breakfasts around the smart dining table; big, bright, high-ceilinged bedrooms with maybe a claw-foot bath, original Georgian shutters or a shiny brass bed. All have spoiling bathrooms. There's a large sitting room downstairs where guests can stretch out in front of the fire, umbrellas in case of rainy days, and a whole list of extras about which I am sworn to secrecy in order to leave room for a few surprises. You are a two-minute walk from the centre of Richmond, it's five minutes to the station for tube and train, and roughly a mile from Richmond Park to the south and Kew Gardens to the north. Ann, who came here via Italy and the Cape, also has green fingers and has brought her courtyard garden to life with busts and statues, a flowering cherry and pots by the dozen.

Rooms: 3: 1 double, 2 twins.
Price: £80-£100.
Meals: Full breakfast included.
Closed: Occasionally.

Train: Richmond (to Waterloo).
Tube: Richmond.
Bus: 33, 190, 337.
Parking: Free off-street.

131 Queens Road

Richmond
TW10 6HF

Tel: 020 8948 6893
Fax: 020 8948 6893

Margaret & Ian Andrew

Margaret and Ian, who have lived all over the world, know their local facts and figures; even though Richmond blood runs in my veins, I had no idea you could take the train to Windsor or the river up to Hampton Court (and thus arrive like Henry VIII). If these destinations sound a little distant, just hop across the road for walks in London's most beautiful park: Richmond. Or jump on the train to Waterloo – it only takes 12 minutes. Back at Number 131, Margaret will advise on where to eat (Chez Maria in the Market Place was causing local waistlines to expand), but you can eat in, too, and in some style. Margaret is a professional cook and with a day's notice she'll conjure up something delicious, maybe home-made coriander and carrot soup, rack of lamb, cold lemon soufflé. After which, climb the stairs in this large Richmond home (1930s pebble dash with leaded bay windows) to your bedroom at the front, a room of blues and yellows – warm as toast, TV, books, blankets, double glazing – for a good night's sleep. Station pick-ups, good conversation and fine breakfasts to start your day.

Rooms: 1 twin, private bathroom.
Price: £60-£70.
Meals: Continental breakfast included, full English £5. Dinner, £30, by arrangement.
Closed: Occasionally.

Train: Richmond (to Waterloo).
Tube: Richmond.
Bus: 33, 337.
Parking: Free off-street.

Map: 3

The Victoria

10 West Temple Sheen
London SW14 7RT

Tel: 020 8876 4238
Fax: 020 8878 3464
E-mail: mark@thevictoria.net
Web: www.thevictoria.net

Mark & Clare Chester

Mark, ex-Conran, now proprietor extraordinaire, was consoling the waitress who had toothache as he made the coffee, his eyes scanning his empire to make sure everything was just so. Which it was: I couldn't see a teaspoon out of place. This is the result of much hard work; last year Mark and Clare transformed the place into a cool, contemporary gastro pub, with airy rooms, wooden floorboards, tongue and groove panelling and purple cushions on the sofas. It's got local tongues wagging, the good folk of Sheen keen to come and try the food. Their efforts will be well-rewarded, the menu appearing as apples did to Eve. Treat yourself to saffron and tomato quiche, Toulouse sausage and mash with onion gravy, and poached pear in red wine, all for £17.50. After which you can retire to stylish bedrooms: white walls, Egyptian cotton, halogen lighting, beechwood beds, goose down pillows, multicoloured blankets and high pressure showers. Great value for money, and with the Sheen Gate entrance to Richmond Park close by, you can walk off your indulgence lost to the world. A great little place.

Rooms: 7: 5 doubles, 2 twin/doubles.
Price: £92.50-£115; singles from £82.50.
Meals: Continental breakfast included. Lunch and dinner £5-£20.
Closed: Never.

Train: Mortlake (to Waterloo).
Bus: 33, 337.
Parking: Free off-street.

Map: 3

Leyden House

Thames Bank
Mortlake
London SW14 7QR

Tel: 020 8876 7375
Fax: 020 8876 6188
E-mail: xrae_leyden@btinternet.com

Rachael Keeling

An impeccable house, one of the finest in this book, with the river Thames lapping ten feet from the front door. I arrived at high tide to find swans pecking at the grass, an oarsman at peace on the water and a half-submerged bench. Inside, you find a treasure-trove country house: a scarlet hall that doubles as a gallery, a dining room (once the billiard room) with wooden floors and gilt mirrors, and, upstairs, a magnificent double drawing room with pillars, bay windows and an open fire at each end. A vibrant house, full of books and art. Second-floor bedrooms are just what you'd hope for. The twin has *bergère* beds, rugs and a small sofa, while the big yellow double is dreamy, with wardrobe, bureau and dresser all elegant mahogany. Look out of the window and watch the odd long boat chug by. Rooms come with bathrobes, electric blankets, carafes of water – a reflection of Rachael's style. Miss Toffee and Tilly, the family dogs, will become firm friends. There's also a large garden with swimming pool and steam bath, and the Thames towpath starts at the front door. A perfect base for those who want to escape the city at night.

Rooms: 3: 1 twin;
2 doubles sharing bathroom
(same-party bookings only).
Price: £90-£110; singles from £50.
Meals: Full breakfast included.
Closed: Occasionally.

Train: Mortlake (to Waterloo).
Bus: 419.
Parking: Free on-street.

Map: 3

1 Charlotte Road

Barnes
London SW13 9QJ

Tel: 020 8741 5504
Fax: 020 8741 5504
E-mail: thegardenpartner@charlotteroad.fsnet.co.uk

Helen Smith

Barnes is London's loveliest village, a throw-back to the 1960s, a place where ducks still live on the village pond opposite a pub where cricketers meet to quench a collective thirst. On one side, towpaths hug each bank of the Thames (the Boat Race passes in March), while on the other, a wild common waits; and between, lovely shops, so beware! As for Helen's immaculate home, it was recently voted one of London's top ten B&Bs. No clutter anywhere, just boundless style: plantation shutters in the large sitting room, where smart red sofas are plumped high with cushions; a shiny wooden floor in the big, bright kitchen, where doors open up to a small garden (for summer breakfasts, if you like). Bedrooms have generous beds, the best linen, fluffy towels – all the spoiling extras. The room at the top has old luggage (the nice stuff that is!), skylights (you can stargaze from bed) and a crisp elegance. The grander double has an Edwardian *bergère* sofa and a purple claw-footed bath in a divine bathroom. Nearby, great restaurants – try Riva, Sonny's or the famous Sun pub – and for a day out, visit the magnificent Wetland Centre.

Rooms: 2 doubles,
1 with private bathroom.
Price: £70-£90; singles from £45.
Meals: Full breakfast included.
Closed: Occasionally.

Train: Barnes or Barnes Bridge
(to Waterloo via Vauxhall).
Tube: Hammersmith (10 minutes by bus).
Bus: 419, 609.
Parking: Free on-street.

Map: 4

11 Queen Anne's Grove

Bedford Park
London W4 1HW

Tel: 020 8995 9255
E-mail: elisabeth.whittaker@virgin.net

Elisabeth Whittaker

Elisabeth knows her stuff and is entertaining and informative: the Battle of Turnham Green (1680), Cromwell's last encounter before he entered London, took place just around the corner in Woodstock Road. Her house is a hotbed of culture, often full of musicians who stay when in town as they can use her music room to practice; it has a Steinway 'A' grand. Elisabeth herself is a sculptor and caster (her work is all around) and she has just managed to get a statue of William Hogarth, a famous local resident, erected nearby. Her quietly stylish home is part of Norman Shaw's 1870s Bedford Park. The top floor is a lovely apartment in country style, with a big open-plan kitchen/sitting room, a very pretty bedroom with crisp white linen, and a cavernous bathroom in blue. Hole up here for a week in London and you will be delighted. There is a big twin on the first floor with books, busts and comfy armchairs. You prepare your own breakfast: Elisabeth stocks up the fridge for your first morning, thereafter you look after yourself. A wonderful spot. Try the old Tabard pub; it has a small theatre above it, too.

Rooms: 2: 1 twin/double; 1 double
in flat with kitchen and sitting room.
Music room by arrangement.
Price: B&B: £60-£70.
Singles from £50.
Flat from £420 per week.
Meals: Continental breakfast provisions
left for you to prepare.
Closed: Never.

Tube: Turnham Green.
Bus: 27, 94, 190, 237.
Parking: Free on-street.

Map: 4

7 Emlyn Road

Stamford Brook
London W12 9TF

Tel: 020 8746 1677
E-mail: rjrichardson@compuserve.com

Sarah & Ricky Richardson

This is the sort of place you see in a glossy magazine and can't quite believe is real, so let me assure you: this is one of London's loveliest B&Bs. Ricky and Sarah have lived all over the world – Upper Volta, Nicaragua, Borneo, Oman, Chiswick – and it is this last port of call that has influenced your suite of rooms; here is crisp English elegance at its best. Beautiful lighting, stencilled beds, fine English linen, original stripped-pine doors, blinds and curtains, a pretty bay window, a small balcony and an Eton burry (a desk from the school); the place is immaculate. You have two rooms, bedroom and sitting room, separated by double doors that you can throw open, thus giving yourself a great sense of space. Lots of pretty bits and bobs about the place – old books, the odd bit of art (Sarah paints), and a huge bathroom with fluffy towels. A continental breakfast is brought up to you the night before and your table set with tablecloths, napkins and fresh flowers; you then help yourself in the morning. The Number 94 stops at the end of the road and takes you all the way to Piccadilly; there's also the tube. A perfect ten.

Rooms: 1 twin/double and sitting room.
Price: £75-£85; singles from £55.
Meals: Continental breakfast included.
Closed: Occasionally.

Tube: Stamford Brook.
Bus: 94.
Parking: Free off-street.

West Central

Brook Green
Shepherd's Bush
Kensington
Holland Park
Notting Hill
Earl's Court
Fulham

Brompton Cemetery

When it's three o'clock in New York,
it's still 1938 in London.

Bette Midler

31 Rowan Road

Brook Green
London W6 7DT

Tel: 020 8748 0930
Fax: 020 8741 4288
E-mail: vickysixsmith@aol.com
Web: www.abetterwaytostay.co.uk

Vicky & Edmund Sixsmith

Terrific value for money in Brook Green, and close to the Thames at Hammersmith for its riverside pubs and walks. Vicky's top-floor pied-à-terre is big and airy, delightfully decorated in greens and yellows with sofas and window seats and a big twin/double bed. You also have a small kitchen (fridge, kettle, toaster, crockery) where you prepare your own continental breakfast whenever you want; it's delivered to you each evening by Leo, Vicky's and Edmund's young son. Also: fresh flowers, pretty floral blinds, an old bureau and a bowl of fresh fruit. Next door (you get the whole of the floor) is a lovely bathroom, with a deep cast-iron bath in which you can lie and gaze out of the skylight at passing traffic, i.e. birds. So, lots of privacy, lots of style and it's a bargain, too, with plenty of space for those on longer stays. On the green itself, tennis courts and the Queen's Head pub with its huge garden, and nearby, great local restaurants: the Havelock (one of London's best gastro pubs), the Gate vegetarian restaurant or the Pope's Eye for serious carnivores.

Rooms: 1 twin/double.
Price: £70-£80; singles from £50.
Meals: Continental breakfast provisions left for you to prepare.
Closed: Occasionally.

Tube: Hammersmith.
Bus: 9, 10, 27, 33.
Parking: £5 a day off-street.

Map: 4

Addison Gardens

Shepherd's Bush
London W14

Tel: 020 7351 3445
Fax: 020 7351 9383
E-mail: inquiries@uptownres.co.uk

Not your run-of-the-mill B&B! Michael's place is wild – but when I read my notes back, I began to wonder if I'd imagined the whole thing. Gold rams? Really? Certainly a claret-and-gold crushed velvet bedcover on a French sleigh bed that's sprinkled with red cherubic cushions and flanked by stone urns that double up as bedside tables. And definitely a spiral staircase corkscrewing though the wooden floor and leading to a bathroom where the cast-iron bath stands free. Candelabra on the marble mantelpiece and gilded cornicing on the ceiling – Michael is a photographer with an eye for funky contemporary style. The room at the top is huge and has a canvas-shaded ceiling, a big sofa and a day bed in one corner. The feel is opulent: bold colours, classical pieces, lots of space, fresh flowers, piles of mags, crisp linen and rug-strewn wooden floors. Breakfast is brought to you: croissants and hot French bread, bowls of fruit and coffee. This vibrant area also has masses of great restaurants. Try Chinon for "outstanding" French food.

Rooms: 2: 1 double; 1 double, private bathroom.
Price: £85-£95; singles from £65.
Meals: Continental breakfast included.
Closed: Occasionally.

Tube: Hammersmith; Shepherd's Bush.
Bus: 9, 10, 27.
Parking: £8 a day on-street.

Map: 4

Holland Road

Kensington
London W14

Tel: 020 7351 3445
Fax: 020 7351 9383
E-mail: inquiries@uptownres.co.uk

Charlotte is a writer and her biography of Hutch, the Black American singer, has just been published. Her 1850's home is huge, with massive rooms. These houses were as grand as could be 100 years ago: this is one of the few to remain so. Lovely things all over the place: masses of cushions on the sofas in the large bay-windowed sitting room, where polished wooden floors lap against a marble fireplace, and lots of art on the walls, brought back from exotic trips. Old oils line the staircase as it curves gently upwards to gigantic bedrooms. The room at the front (some noise from the road, but it's the biggest room I've seen) has two sofas and two armchairs, though you hardly notice them, a massive old brass bed (everything is huge!), books in the bathroom, high ceilings – fabulous. At the back (therefore no noise) a canopied half-tester dominates the room – country-house living in the heart of London. You breakfast downstairs at a farmhouse table in the Aga-warmed kitchen, where doors lead out to the communal garden. A house of art, books and culture, with the cerebral Elizabeth at the helm. Cibo's, the local Italian, is a treat.

Rooms: 2 doubles.
Price: £85-£95; singles from £65.
Meals: Full breakfast included.
Closed: Occasionally.

Tube: Olympia;
High Street Kensington;
Holland Park (all a 10-minute walk).
Bus: 9, 10, 12, 27, 28, 49, 88.
Parking: Nearest car park £25 per 24 hrs.

Map: 4

101 Abbotsbury Road

Holland Park
London W14 8EP

Tel: 020 7602 0179
Fax: 020 7602 1036
E-mail: sunny@101abb.freeserve.co.uk

Sunny Murray

Holland Park is one of London's most sought-after addresses and has been for the last 400 years. Sir Walter Cope built a castle here in 1605 and called it, with breathtaking originality, Cope Castle. His son-in-law, Henry Rich, took over, became the first Earl of Holland, and changed the name to Holland House; so, not a vain bunch at all. Sunny's gorgeous family home is right opposite the park (you can bird-watch in its woods) and is well-placed for High Street Kensington, Notting Hill and Olympia. The whole top floor is generally given over to guests. Both rooms have been beautifully decorated in gentle yellows and greens, with pale green carpets, soft white duvets, pelmeted windows and a lovely, curved chest of drawers in the double bedroom. There are big porcelain table lights, an old Robert's radio, fresh flowers and treetop views. The bathroom is marble-tiled and sky-lit, with a deep cast-iron bath; great comfort is guaranteed. Breakfast is taken continental-style in the kitchen. You're near to Kensington Gardens, and the Number 9 or Number 10 bus will drop you off at the Albert Hall, Knightsbridge or Piccadilly.

Rooms: 2: 1 double and 1 single
sharing bathroom.
Price: £80-£90; singles from £45.
Meals: Continental breakfast included.
Closed: Occasionally.

Tube: Holland Park.
Bus: 9, 10, 27, 28, 94.
Parking: Off-street by arrangement.

Map: 4

Portobello Hotel

22 Stanley Gardens
London W11 2NG

Tel: 020 7727 2777
Fax: 020 7792 9641
E-mail: info@portobello-hotel.co.uk
Web: www.portobello-hotel.co.uk

Hanna Turner

The Portobello is to funky London hotels what Elvis is to rock and roll: the original. The hotel opened in 1970, a groovy response to groovy times, signalling a fundamental shift in attitudes from what was a decidedly formal world. It became *the* place to stay in London, for artists and musicians, film stars and designers, and it still is, with a star-studded list of regulars who come for its seductive combination of privacy and informality and the opulence of its rooms. You can sleep in a four-poster from Hampton Court Palace, refresh yourself in a brass-piped Victorian shower, recline on a curved sofa that was made to fit the room, or revitalise yourself in a steam bath. Cool, colonial interiors run throughout. Wander at will and you find ferns potted in an ancient thunder-box, a three-foot-deep gilded claw-foot bath, or Chinese sofas in a tiny dining room. The Japanese room, in bamboo and marble, has a small conservatory with doors out to a tiny courtyard garden where walls are tiled with sea shells. You can eat here or at nearby Julie's, another Notting Hill institution, owned (and cooked) by the same people. Don't miss it.

Rooms: 24: 12 special rooms, 5 doubles, 2 twins and 5 singles.
Price: £185-£200; special rooms £240-£320; singles £140.
Meals: Continental breakfast included; full English £8.50. Lunch and dinner, £18-£20 for 2 courses. Room service.
Closed: 23 December-3 January.

Tube: Notting Hill Gate.
Bus: 12, 27, 28, 52, 70, 94.
Parking: Nearest car park £25 per 24 hrs.

Map: 1

Portobello Gold

95-97 Portobello Road
Notting Hill
London W11 2QB

Tel: 020 7460 4910
Fax: 020 7229 2278
E-mail: mike@portobellogold.com
Web: www.portobellogold.com

Michael Bell & Linda Johnson-Bell

Bill Clinton popped in for lunch a couple of years back, chatted with the locals, downed a pint, then left without paying. He inhaled – the Portobello air, that is – as you can, too, while sitting out on the pavement watching local life pass by. Wake up on Saturdays and find the market right outside the door. And you can stay here for London's equivalent of next to nothing. Rooms are clean but fairly basic: if you're after fancy hotel luxury then this is not for you. But if that doesn't matter, there's a conservatory/jungle dining room at the back (book the cushioned hippy deck), tiled floors and open fires in the bar, and good art on the walls (the place doubles as a gallery); a cyber café, free to hotel guests, and Michael will even put a PC in your room for 24-hour surfing; trappist ales, Belgian beers and the best wines available by the glass (Linda is a wine writer); superb food (Thai moules, sashimi, Irish rock oysters); friendly natives; and a Rolls Royce minicab service. There's a great suite with private roof terrace if you do want a bit of luxury. Carnival comes in August; watch it pass from the roof.

Rooms: 6: 2 doubles; 2 doubles and 1 single each with shower, sharing wc; 1 suite.
Price: £55-£95; singles £50-£60; suite £180.
Meals: Continental breakfast included, full English £5.50. Bar meals from £6. Lunch and dinner, £10-£25. Room service.
Closed: Never.

Tube: Notting Hill.
Bus: 12, 27, 28, 31, 52, 328.
Parking: Nearest car park £25 per 24 hrs.

Map: 1 30

Miller's

111a Westbourne Grove
London W2 4UW

Tel: 020 7243 1024
Fax: 020 7243 1064
E-mail: enquiries@millersuk.com
Web: www.millersuk.com

Martin Miller

This is Miller's, as in the antique guides, and the collectibles on show in the first-floor drawing room make it one of the great spots in London for undemanding hedonists. The week I visited, guests included Marianne Faithful, the top brass of a Milan fashion house, a professional gambler and an opera singer who was giving guests lessons. Breakfast is taken communally around a 1920s walnut table in a drawing room where, at ten o'clock on the morning I visited, a fire was smouldering in a huge carved-wood fireplace. You get an idea of what to expect when you step in off the street and pass an 18th-century sedan chair stuffed under the stairs, as if discarded, but in the drawing room, to give you a taster: a gilt-framed Sony Trinitron, a Tibetan deity (well, his statue), a 1750s old master's chair, a couple of hundred candles, flower pots embedded with oranges, a samurai sword, busts and sculptures, oils by the score, globes, chandeliers, plinths, rugs, sofas... Aladdin was a pauper if you compare his cave to this one. Bedrooms upstairs are equally embellished, just a little less cluttered. Perfection never came so cheap.

Rooms: 6 doubles.
Price: £140-£195.
Meals: Continental breakfast included.
Closed: Never.

Tube: Bayswater;
Queensway;
Notting Hill Gate.
Bus: 7, 23, 28, 31, 70.
Parking: Nearest car park £25 per 24 hrs.

Pembroke Square

Kensington
London W8

Tel: 020 7351 3445
Fax: 020 7351 9383
E-mail: inquiries@uptownres.co.uk

A delightful 1840s square that gets much more light than next-door Edwardes Square (which the locals all think is prettier). If you want to judge for yourself, walk to its famous pub, the Scarsdale, sit with your drink in its verdant front garden and muse upon it. However, once you return to your family home you will care not a jot, especially while you recline on the *chaise longue* at the end of your bed, and gaze out through Georgian windows onto the quiet life of a London square. Or pop on a video from owner Christine's collection (*Gone with the Wind*, *Casablanca*, *Some like it Hot*) and nod off. This is a very spoiling house, with Christine the main spoiler. On the day I visited she had just finished making her cranberry sauce and Christmas puddings; breakfast may include banana and pecan nut muffins. There's a sitting room you're welcome to use, but you may not need it as the bedroom is substantial: two original ceiling-to-floor windows, lots of storage space, the *chaise longue* and books that include Zelda Fitzgerald's short stories. You can play tennis in the square and Kensington High Street is close.

Rooms: 1 twin/double.
Price: £85-£95; singles £65.
Meals: Continental breakfast included.
Closed: Occasionally.

Tube: High Street Kensington;
Earl's Court.
Bus: 9, 10, 27, 28, 31.
Parking: High Street Kensington car park
£25 per 24 hrs.

Map: 4

Amsterdam Hotel

7 Trebovir Road
Earl's Court
London SW5 9LS

Tel: 020 7370 2814
Fax: 020 7244 7608
E-mail: reservations@amsterdam-hotel.com
Web: www.amsterdam-hotel.com

Judith Verrier

The Amsterdam is a good find, tucked away in an Earl's Court back street, close to the tube, and very well priced. First and foremost, it is absolutely spotless, with an army of maids who blitz it daily, top to bottom. Another boon is the size of the bedrooms: either big or fairly big. They are also highly idiosyncratic, decorated in bright, bold colours: yellow and blue, purple and orange, blue and green, always a combination that clothes the room, with acres of curtain that tumble from the ceiling. There are good bathrooms, not huge, but entirely adequate, TVs, ample lighting, wicker and bamboo furniture. Singles all have double beds and the triples or two-bedded suites are very reasonable too. There's a garden at the back, internet access, a small jungle of ferns in reception, lots of mirrors on the walls, and downstairs, in the basement, a pretty yellow breakfast room with wooden floors. A very cheerful place. Earl's Court is a one-minute walk away, as is the tube, and if you want somewhere to stroll, try the enchanting Brompton Cemetery close by.

Rooms: 27: 9 twin/doubles,
4 singles, 6 family, 8 suites.
Price: £90-£105; singles from £80;
suites £115-£160.
Meals: Continental breakfast included,
full English £3.
Closed: Never.

Tube: Earl's Court.
Bus: 28, 31, 74, 328, C1.
Parking: Warwick Road car park
£20 per 24 hrs.

Map: 4

Twenty Nevern Square

Earl's Court
London SW5 9PD

Tel: 020 7565 9555
Fax: 020 7565 9444
E-mail: hotel@twentynevernsquare.co.uk
Web: www.twentynevernsquare.co.uk

Aleksandra Turner

A smart red-brick exterior with terracotta urns guarding the steps and an arched porch at the front door. This is a great little place, a fusion of classical and minimalist styles, with a clean, cool interior and beautiful things all around: Victorian birdcages, gilt mirrors, porcelain vases, a bowl full of dried rose petals. There's a real flow to the downstairs, all the way though to the conservatory-restaurant, with its stained glass, ceiling fans, hanging ferns, wicker chairs and glass tables. Bedrooms are equally stylish, with natural colours on the walls, cedar-wood blinds and rich fabrics throughout: silks, cottons and linens – nothing here is synthetic. CD players and TVs have been cleverly hidden away in pretty wooden cabinets; there is no clutter. Rooms come in different shapes and sizes, each with something to elate: an Indonesian hand-carved wooden headboard, an Egyptian sleigh bed, a colonial four-poster, some sweeping blue and gold silk curtains. There are marble bathrooms, too. Great value for money, very friendly staff, and close to the tube.

Rooms: 20: 13 doubles, 3 twins, 3 four-posters and 1 suite.
Price: £110-£140; four-posters from £150; suite from £190; singles £80-£110.
Meals: Continental breakfast included, full English £5-£9. Dinner, 2 courses, from £10. Room service.
Closed: Never.

Tube: Earl's Court.
Bus: 74, 328, C1, C3.
Parking: £17 a day off-street.

Map: 4

Hartismere Road

Fulham
London SW6 7TS

Tel: 020 7385 0337
Fax: 020 7385 0337

Joan Lee

Joan is something of a globe-trotter, and the last couple of years have seen her in Namibia, Botswana, Finland, Estonia, China and by the Black Sea. Over coffee, the photo albums came out and we oohed and aahed our way around the world. She knows Fulham, too, and will tell you where to eat (Miragio's is fabulous) and what to see (the North End Road Market – more cockneys than East Enders). Her 1880s worker's cottage is swamped in summer by a rambling 'Mermaid' rose, pale yellow and easy on the eye. You enter at the side of the house, straight into the big, open-plan kitchen/dining room, a room full of books and plants. The table here hosts what I expect are extremely convivial breakfasts, which include apple compotes, croissants, home-made jams and marmalades. Upstairs, two bedrooms: a smallish, well-furnished double, and a delightful yellow single at the back of the house, with rugs, books and a mahogany dresser; both have electric blankets for the odd chilly night. If you want to see a little bit of hidden London, go and visit the war graves in Fulham cemetery, just off Munster Road.

Rooms: 2: 1 double and 1 single sharing bathroom.
Price: £70; singles £45-£50.
Meals: Continental breakfast included.
Closed: Occasionally.

Tube: Fulham Broadway.
Bus: 11, 14, 28, 295.
Parking: £8 a day on-street.

8 Hartismere Road

Fulham
London SW6 7TT

Tel: 020 7381 8128
E-mail: jgsulimir@aol.com

George & Diana Pearson

Like London buses: you wait for a good B&B to come along, then two turn up in the same street. Diana and George have lived in Fulham for 25 years, the last couple of them here. George, who is originally from Kraków, now runs a backgammon club, so if you're a Polish-speaking backgammon player... This is a pretty house, very homely, with a big sitting room in racing red at the front (they knocked down a wall to open things up) and an open-plan kitchen/dining room looking onto the small courtyard garden at the back. Here Diana serves breakfast or, with a bit of notice, supper (Thai curry, a Polish casserole, that sort of thing). The bedroom is upstairs at the front of the house, with a Victorian mahogany desk, comfy beds, colourful curtains and good luggage space. There are bathrobes, too, and a sparkling bathroom three paces from your bedroom door. Fulham life, with its cafés and restaurants, is a short stroll, and Queen's tennis tournament, the precursor to Wimbledon (and popular with the top players), takes place close by in the first two weeks of June.

Rooms: 1 twin with private bathroom.
Price: £70-£80; singles from £45.
Meals: Continental breakfast included. Dinner, by arrangement, £12.50.
Closed: Occasionally.

Tube: Fulham Broadway.
Bus: 11, 14, 28, 211, 295.
Parking: £8 a day on-street.

Map: 4

36

29 Winchendon Road

Fulham
London SW6 5DH

Tel: 020 7731 3901
E-mail: rachel.k.wilson@talk21.com

Rachel Wilson

You walk through the front door and know you've chosen well. Rachel is one of those people who gives generously and thinks nothing of it; it's her instinct to be kind. The house glows warm gold as you enter, courtesy of Osborne & Little on the walls, and excellent halogen lighting. Upstairs, an exceptionally pretty double with pink checks, bright whites and garden views, fresh flowers, floral prints, and a sparkling bathroom, too. The hub of the house is back downstairs in the kitchen, where you can sit upon the sofa, or open up the French windows and enjoy the serenity of a small London garden. On sunny mornings you can breakfast out here under the parasol, with the passion flower and clematis trailing the walls that surround you. The street runs down to the Fulham Road, where you will find the lovely Nomad bookshop, Bridgewater pottery (bring the kids, design your own) and the linen-and-lavender shop, Cologne & Cotton. There are lots of restaurants close by including the Loch Fyne Fish Restaurant, the new boy on the street. Good bus and tube connections, too. Immaculate.

Rooms: 3: 1 double; 1 twin and 1 single, both with private bathrooms.
Price: £70-£90; singles from £45.
Meals: Continental breakfast included.
Closed: Occasionally.

Tube: Parsons Green.
Bus: 14.
Parking: £8 a day on-street.

Map: 4

Crondace Road

Fulham
London SW6

Tel: 020 7351 3445
Fax: 020 7351 9383
E-mail: inquiries@uptownres.co.uk

A duck-egg-blue Fulham house that looks over a thin strip of Eel Brook Common to the New King's Road beyond. Walk in off the street and you are seduced immediately: a big gilt mirror in the hall, a long Irish farmhouse table in the dining room, a couple of carved swans by the French windows and warm lighting, yellow walls and an elegant family-house feel. Tennis rackets and umbrellas by the front door, a bookshelf full of guides in the dining room. Pretty bedrooms have crisp linen and fresh flowers, TVs and lovely duvets. The one at the back is smaller but has garden views and the bigger bathroom; the one at the front under the eaves has what little noise the road may throw up (which isn't much at night) and a small tub bath and power shower. It also has a small single across the way, thus good for families as they get the whole floor to themselves. All are spotless. Parsons Green tube is close by and if you want to eat locally at night, there are three good restaurants within 50 paces of the front door.

Rooms: 3: 1 twin/double;
1 twin/double and 1 double
sharing tub bath and shower
(same-party bookings only).
Price: £85-£95; singles from £65.
Meals: Continental breakfast included.
Closed: Occasionally.

Tube: Parsons Green.
Bus: 22.
Parking: £8 a day on-street.

Map: 4

3 Bradbourne Street

Fulham
London SW6 3TF

Tel: 020 7736 7284
E-mail: info@luxuryinlondon.clara.co.uk
Web: www.luxuryinlondon.co.uk

Amanda Turner

A handsome 1880s red-brick house just around the corner from the New King's Road and less than a minute's walk from Parsons Green. Stroll across it and you come to the famous White Horse pub, where you can eat and drink like a king. Amanda's home has echoes of India, with elephant wallpaper in the upstairs double and prints on the wall in the hall. But beyond the indisputable comforts of her home – and there are many – Amanda's attention to detail and her happy way of doing things are what make the place so special. Harrods' jams and pancakes for breakfast, either in the kitchen or the garden; candles everywhere; and Huggy the dog, an erstwhile star of the silver screen, who turned down the movies and the promise of a chauffeured limousine for the quiet life in Fulham. The downstairs bedroom is lovely: big and bright, warm and airy and excellent for longer stays, the Italian-tiled bathroom next door just the ticket. A great little place, a home-from-home in the city, and Amanda will book tables in restaurants and generally advise. The green hosts a fête in June.

Rooms: 2 twin/doubles, 1 with private bathroom.
Price: £75; singles £55.
Meals: Continental breakfast included.
Closed: Occasionally.

Tube: Parsons Green.
Bus: 22.
Parking: £8 a day on-street.

Map: 4

34 Wandsworth Bridge Road

Fulham   **Tel:** 020 7731 2805
London SW6 2TH   **Fax:** 020 7731 2805

Sally Usher

Sally's governess, one Tatiana Yorkavitch, taught her nothing other than how to sweeten her tea with jam... which, 40 years later, she still occasionally does. What this house lacks in style on the outside it makes up for amply within. Sally has a good eye and her yellow drawing room is something of an Aladdin's cave: beautiful 18th-century French chairs (one is made of papier-mâché), gilt mirrors, hat stands, raw silk blinds, family pics and the odd oil on the wall. Classical music wafts about the place. Don't expect the ordinary – this house is undeniably flamboyant, the nail-varnish-pink bathroom quite wild. Bedrooms are cool, cream, clutter-free: swathes of curtain in the large lower-ground double, paintings by a Russian friend in the smaller upper-ground one. Breakfast is served in the kitchen / dining room, with pink napkins, fresh flowers and a tall gilt candlestick lit at breakfast. Sally is well-travelled; she organises tours in London and throughout Britain, so is full of ideas. If you want to eat Thai in some style, try Jim Thompson's on the New King's Road.

Rooms: 2 doubles,
1 with private bathroom.
Price: £60-£70; singles £40-£50.
Meals: Continental breakfast included.
Closed: Never.

Tube: Fulham Broadway.
Bus: 11, 22, 28, 295.
Parking: £8 a day on-street.

30 Stokenchurch Street

Fulham
London SW6 3TR

Tel: 020 7731 2281
Fax: 020 7731 2281
E-mail: butler.c.j@talk21.com

Jenny Butler

Jenny, who overflows with life, has spent the last two years renovating and chivvying builders and carpet layers into meeting deadlines. And a good thing too, for us at least, for her house is now ready for your pleasure... you will find much. The interior has been decorated in warm yellows, giving it a mellow feel. It's a smart place, well-lit, with a lovely dining room at the front into which morning sunlight steals through an impressive window of arches and squares. Upstairs, smart country-style bedrooms pile on the luxuries: thick blankets, old dressers, antique furniture, fresh flowers, sheets or duvets, whichever you want. (Whatever you're allergic to, they've got the alternative.) Tea or coffee is brought to your room: great service given generously with a genuine smile. Bathrooms are excellent, too, with deep cast-iron baths, and two have Grohr showers (the best, apparently). The super single at the back is a gem, and bucks the trend for single people paying inflated prices for inferior rooms in London. Breakfast is a feast. Jenny is a natural host and looks after you exceptionally well.

Rooms: 4: 1 twin and 1 double,
each with private bathroom;
1 double and 1 single sharing bathroom.
Price: £65-£80; singles £45.
Meals: Full breakfast included.
Closed: Never.

Tube: Parsons Green.
Bus: 22, 28, 295.
Parking: £8 a day on-street.

8 Parthenia Road

Fulham
London SW6 3BD

Tel: 020 7384 1165
Fax: 020 7610 6015
E-mail: carolinedocker@angelwings.co.uk

Caroline & George Docker

A smart London-brick house, hidden at the front by a well-trimmed box hedge that George keeps in fine order. Your room is at the top of the house: four short flights of stairs await, but your reward is well worth the effort as you find a sumptuous room, decorated beautifully in country-house style (Caroline is an interior designer): an old oak table, a plush armchair, wonderfully heavy curtains, the crispest of linen sheets – heavenly stuff. There's loads of storage space and a pretty shower room, though if you'd like a bathroom, you can have one down on the landing (and like the rest of the house, it is crammed with beautiful art). Come all the way down again for breakfast at that old oak table in the dining room, where portraits of a couple of ancestors hang on the walls. There's a small, pretty brick garden, full of colour in summer, where you can have your croissants and coffee, a delight on fine mornings. Caroline mixes the sophistication of the city with the human warmth of the countryside – this is a great place to stay. The King's Road boutiques and antiques are close by.

Rooms: 1 twin/double.
Price: £80-£100; singles £70.
Meals: Continental breakfast included.
Closed: Never.

Tube: Parsons Green.
Bus: 14, 22.
Parking: £8 a day on-street.

Map: 4

42

Barclay Road

Fulham
London SW6

Tel: 020 7351 3445
Fax: 020 7351 9383
E-mail: inquiries@uptownres.co.uk

Charlotte, a Bostonian at home in London, is great fun – relaxed and relaxing. Guests bring out her natural flamboyance (she does something unspeakably high-powered by day) and keep her human. You get jazz at breakfast in the huge wooden-floored dining/sitting room, served at a table next to a grand piano. Twist Charlotte's arm and she'll play for you – she's a frustrated musician, a much better one than she'd ever admit. She's generous, too, and gives you your own sitting room with an open fire, leather sofas, wooden floors and lots of London guides. Next door is the bedroom, smallish but well laid out, with internet access, picket-fenced window boxes on the ledge, fresh flowers, seagrass matting and William Morris fabrics. There are waffle bathrobes – a present from the concièrge at the Chicago Four Seasons – and a lovely bathroom (you'll think you're in a library) with a deep bath, a tartan carpet and a huge mirror. And... there are two roof terraces, one at treetop level where you can take a sundowner. An easy-going place and a great London find.

Rooms: 1 double, private bathroom.
Price: £85-£95; singles from £65.
Meals: Continental breakfast included.
Closed: Occasionally.

Tube: Fulham Broadway.
Bus: 14, 28, 295.
Parking: £8 a day on-street.

Map: 4

Britannia Road

Fulham
London SW6

Tel: 020 7351 3445
Fax: 020 7351 9383
E-mail: inquiries@uptownres.co.uk

The day I visited, Claire and John had just returned from a holiday under an Australian sun, and though London lay under a blanket of cloud, the bright, creamy yellow interior that runs throughout their home was the perfect antidote to the winter blues. Step off a quiet, residential street (it is barred to passing traffic) and you are met with crisp, uncluttered elegance: big sofas to sink into, an ornate wooden fireplace, good carpets and shelves of well-ordered books. Upstairs, a very pretty bedroom, with purple tulips bursting from a vase, masses of storage space, an antique dresser and a bowl of pebbles collected from beaches around the world. Also, crisply-laundered sheets and duvet covers, towels on the towel rail, and a good bathroom with both bath and power shower. There is one more bedroom in the same style on the second floor, let on special request. Breakfast either at the dining room table or, in good weather, outside on the deck above the water garden. The tube is a one-minute walk; wander a little further and you'll find the antique shops of Lillie Road, Bishop's Park, and the Thames at Putney Bridge.

Rooms: 2: 1 double;
1 double sharing bathroom and shower.
Price: £85-£95; singles from £65.
Meals: Continental breakfast included.
Closed: Occasionally.

Tube: Fulham Broadway.
Bus: 14, 22.
Parking: £10 a day on-street.

South Central

Chelsea
South Kensington
Pimlico
Sloane Square
Knightsbridge
Victoria
Mayfair
St James's

Kensington Gardens

Hearts just as pure and fair
May beat in Belgrave Square
As in the lowly air
Of Seven Dials.

W. S. Gilbert, 'Iolanthe'

6 Oakfield Street

Little Chelsea
London SW10 9JB

Tel: 020 7352 2970
E-mail: demare@easynet.co.uk

Margaret & Simon de Maré

Margaret and Simon take it in turns to cook breakfast at the weekends so they can each be sure of a lie-in! This district of Little Chelsea dates from the mid-1660s and Simon, who knows his Chelsea onions, has maps to prove it. He can tell you where Queen Elizabeth I sheltered from the rain, or where Sir Thomas More lived. He also makes delightfully eccentric collages that hang on the walls. Enter their 1860s house and you glimpse a collection of Egyptian prints – they once lived in Cairo. There's an open-plan feel to the kitchen, a marble-topped table in the dining room, and a second-floor roof terrace where you can sit in summer under a smart green umbrella. You can have bacon and eggs for breakfast, then hop on the Number 14 bus to Piccadilly – perfect; they also do a mean cup of coffee. Bedrooms are at the top of the house. The twin, in blue and yellow, is smaller than the double, but being at the back is silent at night. The double has a big wooden bed and an 18th-century oak *armoire*. Restaurants on Hollywood Road are a 30-second stroll and close by is Brompton Cemetery, well worth discovering.

Rooms: 2: 1 double, 1 twin.
Price: £60-£70; singles £40-£50.
Meals: Full breakfast included.
Closed: Occasionally.

Tube: Earl's Court (15-minute walk).
Bus: 14.
Parking: Nearest car park £25 per 24 hrs.

Map: 4

Old Church Street

Chelsea
London SW3

Tel: 020 7351 3445
Fax: 020 7351 9383
E-mail: inquiries@uptownres.co.uk

If you see the dining room first, you'll want to camp in it! It is panelled on all sides, but the old ship's-timber panelling predates this Grade II, 1914, Arts-and-Crafts-style house by a couple of hundred years – rare in a London home. There's also a rather grand oil on the wall (Clair, the owner, will tell you of whom) and a screen by the window to protect you from passing eyes while you eat your cornflakes. The rest of the house is more contemporary: shiny wooden floors, some arched windows, white walls, a "family throne", and, on the first floor, a music room, with a harp five foot high and a grand piano. The bedroom is at the front of the house and has a king-size double and a single bed. It's a big room with rugs on a wooden floor, crisp linen, two armchairs and lots of mirrors. A glorious bathroom waits next door, decorated with blue-green mosaics. You're in the middle of Chelsea, a one-minute walk from the King's Road, or you can walk across Albert Bridge and be in Battersea Park in under ten. Good pubs and restaurants close by; try the ever-popular Front Page, or the Phene Arms with its lovely summer garden.

Rooms: 1 family for 3.
Price: £85-£95; singles from £65.
Meals: Continental breakfast included, full English £5.
Closed: Occasionally.

Tube: Sloane Square (15-minute walk).
Bus: 11, 19, 22, 49, 211, 319.
Parking: Nearest car park £25 per 24 hrs.

   **Map: 5**

Elm Park Gardens

Chelsea
London SW3

Tel: 020 7351 3445
Fax: 020 7351 9383
E-mail: inquiries@uptownres.co.uk

A turn-of-the-century mansion block just behind the Chelsea Arts Club, with a large, plush bedroom and access to one of those big communal gardens so adored by the lucky Londoners that have them. Maggie, a fitness instructor, serves breakfast (pains au chocolat, croissants, fruit, the odd organic egg) in a Mediterranean-style conservatory, where doors lead out to the terracotta pots of a small private garden. The big, bright bedroom at the back of the house (more garden views) is spotless. You'll find crisp linen, orange woollen blankets, halogen lighting and cushions piled up on the bed. Best of all is the fabulous marble bathroom with deep bath, a wall of mirror, big white towels, heated towel rails and "the most powerful shower ever," to quote a hundred former guests. Maggie and Peter are easy-going, keen for you to have as much privacy as you please. They know the area well and will advise you, but you're between the Fulham Road and the King's Road, so you can pretty much follow your nose and not get lost. Good antique shops are close by as is the Anglesea, which does great food.

Rooms: 1 double.
Price: £85-£95; singles from £65.
Meals: Continental breakfast included.
Closed: Occasionally.

Tube: Gloucester Road (12-minute walk).
Bus: 11, 14, 19, 22, 211, 319, 345.
Parking: Nearest car park £25 per 24 hrs.

Map: 5

Aster House

3 Sumner Place
South Kensington
London SW7 3EE

Tel: 020 7581 5888
Fax: 020 7584 4925
E-mail: AsterHouse@btinternet.com
Web: www.AsterHouse.com

Simon & Leonie Tan

The small water garden out back is something of a duck-magnet: wild ducks come to breed in spring, and a couple have made it their permanent residence. A very welcoming small hotel in South Kensington with an unexpectedly beautiful, first-floor conservatory breakfast room that looks out over Sumner Place, giving a bird's eye view of passing life while you polish off your croissants and scrambled eggs. The room has a high, vaulted-glass ceiling and is shielded from the sun by bamboo blinds; ferns tumble from Victorian brass light fittings at the side. Not a place stuffed with antiques, but a very comfortable base none the less. Smart red carpets run throughout and bedrooms come with lots of trimmings: air conditioning, marble bathrooms and orthopaedic mattresses. Also, fresh flowers, pretty fabrics, plush carpets, halogen lighting – some rooms even have crowns above the beds. One room at the back has French windows that open onto the garden. Lots of local restaurants: San Frediano's is fifty yards away, and the nearby Builder's Arms does excellent gastro pub food. Come in January when rooms cost £99 for two.

Rooms: 14: 10 twin/doubles, 3 singles and 1 four-poster.
Price: £135-£180; singles £75-£99.
Meals: Continental breakfast included.
Closed: Never.

Tube: South Kensington.
Bus: 14.
Parking: Nearest car park £25 per 24 hrs.

Hyde Park Gate

Kensington
London SW7 5DH

Tel: 020 7584 9404
Fax: 020 7584 9404

Jasmyne Davoudi

Winston Churchill lived in this street, as did Epstein, while Virginia Woolfe grew up in this actual house (now five flats). This illustrious hall of fame has much to do with the position of the road, a cul-de-sac on the Knightsbridge/Kensington border, a one-minute stroll from Kensington Gardens. Walk to the end of the road (30 seconds), pick up the Number Nine bus and let it chauffeur you to Piccadilly. Only after Jasmyne has cooked you a delicious breakfast, though; she looks after guests generously. You have the room at the back, sweetly decorated in coral, with fresh flowers, the head of the bed in an alcove, and lots of space. Books and magazines, too; your private loo doubles as a library. Back to breakfast: Jasmyne spoils you rotten. You get the full works (bacon, eggs and grilled tomatoes, or smoked salmon and scrambled eggs on Sundays), served on the family china by the window at a mahogany dining table. Lots of good restaurants nearby, and, if you want, you can walk through parks all the way to Buckingham Palace, Westminster, Oxford Street or Notting Hill.

Rooms: 1 double, private wc.
Price: £70-£90; singles £50.
Meals: Full breakfast included.
Closed: Occasionally.

Tube: Gloucester Road.
Bus: 9, 10, 52.
Parking: Nearest car park £25 per 24 hrs.

Map: 4

49

Imperial College London

Watts Way
Princes Gardens
South Kensington
London SW7 1LU

Tel: 020 7594 9507
Fax: 020 7594 9504
E-mail: accommodationlink@ic.ac.uk
Web: www.imperialcollege-conferencelink.com

Michael Cheung

Here's something outstanding. Two hundred paces from the Albert Hall, the campus accommodation of Imperial College (five Nobel prizewinners; famous alumnus: Sir Alexander Fleming) is open to all during the Easter and summer holidays. If you want proof that students have an easy life, then here's the pudding. I saw Beit Hall (pictured) – a thoroughly decent place, where rooms are big and bright, recently decorated, spotlessly clean, nothing to complain about. Some have views of the Hall's dome. You can opt for a room with a shower, or walk up the corridor to private bathrooms and pay less (£60 for two in the heart of London). Extraordinarily, they keep the whole place running for you: the cafeterias, the sports centre (swimming, tennis, squash), the bars (subsidised beer). There's a full cleaning service, linen and towels are all thrown in – I can't emphasise enough how nice the place is. You can stroll about, see the quads, the Queen's Tower, the college gardens. All the big museums are around the corner (Imperial owns the land) and Hyde Park is on your doorstep. Great for the Proms (August/September).

Rooms: 1,196: mix of twins and singles, some with showers, others sharing baths and showers.
Price: £59-£76; singles from £39.50.
Meals: Breakfast included. Lunch and dinner from £5.
Closed: Open during Easter and summer holidays.

Tube: South Kensington.
Bus: 9, 10, 14, 52, 74, C1.
Parking: Nearest car park £25 per 24 hrs.

Map: 5

20 Bywater Street

Chelsea
London SW3 4XD

Tel: 020 7581 2222
Fax: 020 7581 2222
E-mail: caheatonw@aol.com

Caroline & Richard Heaton-Watson

Another great find. Bywater Street is a cul-de-sac off the King's Road – soundproofed, yet close to the shops. It's also one of those London streets where residents paint their houses in pastel colours, thus creating an architectural rainbow. Incredibly, these were workmen's houses when built in 1857. Now they are as desirable as any you'll find in London (John Le Carré let Smilie live here). Richard and Caroline are extremely welcoming, give tea or coffee on arrival, then pass on all the local secrets. The bedroom is downstairs, a pretty room, spotlessly clean, with warm lighting, stripes and checks, a brand new carpet and a wicker chair. Breakfast is across the hall in the kitchen/conservatory, a bright and cheery room that swims in morning sun. Doors open onto a smallish paved garden full of terracotta pots. Sloane Square is a five-minute walk, King's Road is at the top of the street. Try the Coopers Arms for both good food and fine ale. An exceptionally peaceful central London base.

Rooms: 1 double, private shower.
Price: £80-£90; singles from £50.
Meals: Continental breakfast included.
Closed: Occasionally.

Tube: Sloane Square.
Bus: 11, 19, 22, 137, 211.
Parking: Nearest car park £25 per 24 hrs.

Number Ninety-Six

96 Tachbrook Street
Pimlico
London SW1V 2NB

Tel: 020 7932 0969
Fax: 020 7821 5454
E-mail: helen@numberninety-six.co.uk
Web: www.numberninety-six.co.uk

Mrs Helen Douglas

This is great value for money – a tremendously spoiling place and very private. You get the run of the basement: your own entrance, a lovely bathroom in the vaulted old coal cellar, a sitting room big enough to swallow two seven-foot sofas and a king-size four-poster in the bedroom. Jenny, the housekeeper, has been here over 30 years and brings breakfast to you: freshly-squeezed orange juice, hot croissants, fresh rolls and brown toast, with home-made jams and marmalade, and a newspaper, too. Rooms have great style: gilt-framed mirrors, porcelain lamps, heavy curtains, plush carpets, and I counted 16 pictures in the sitting room. There are books in the bookcase and big white towels on the heated towel rail. And that rarity in London – lots of space! Victoria is a five-minute walk, Pimlico tube only two. Keep going and you soon come to Tate Britain, The Houses of Parliament, Westminster Abbey, St James's Park, Buckingham Palace. A very special place in the heart of London.

Rooms: 1 four-poster with sitting room and bathroom.
Price: £110-£120; singles £100.
Meals: Continental breakfast included, full English £8.
Closed: Occasionally.

Tube: Pimlico.
Bus: 2, 24, 36 and others.
Parking: Rochester Row car park £25 per 24 hrs.

The Sloane Hotel

29 Draycott Place
Chelsea
London SW3 2SH

Tel: 020 7581 5757
Fax: 020 7584 1348
E-mail: reservations@sloanehotel.com
Web: www.sloanehotel.com

Miguel Pita

You get an inkling of what to expect at the Sloane by walking into its reception hall: a faux leopard-skin sofa, a mountain of vintage luggage, an ancient admiral's uniform, a gilded marble fireplace and a huge cabinet in one corner with ornate columns and pediment; nothing in the room is less than breathtaking. Nor, for that matter, is the rest of the hotel. On our tour we stopped first in a bedroom with a mirrored wall behind an 18th-century walnut bed, with rich claret wallpaper and 16 pictures on one wall. It was an extraordinary room (a standard double), so I asked if people often described it as "opulent". "Not this one, but the others, yes", came the reply. And things do get more opulent. I saw nowhere quite like the Sloane in my travels; it is a treasure-trove of beautiful things. Look out for faux fur blankets, four-poster beds draped in raw silk, antiques that span five centuries, exquisite *Lelièvre* wallpaper, porcelain pots, armchairs and sofas dressed in the finest fabrics; the place is an A-Z of designers old and new. There's a twist, too – you can buy the lot. The beds, apparently, are extremely popular. Amazing.

Rooms: 22: 16 doubles, 6 suites.
Price: £175-£250; suites from £280.
Meals: Full breakfast £9-£12.
Room service.
Closed: Never.

Tube: Sloane Square.
Bus: 11, 19, 22, 137, 211, C1.
Parking: Nearest car park £21 per 24 hrs.

Map: 5

The London Outpost

69 Cadogan Gardens
Sloane Square
London SW3 2RB

Tel: 020 7589 7333
Fax: 020 7581 4958
E-mail: londonoutpost@dial.pipex.com

Caroline Nolan

This little enclave around Sloane Square is full of spoiling hotels, with none more spoiling than the Outpost. It is the London residence of the Carnegie Club, whose main base is the magnificent Skibo castle, where Madonna married. Here in SW3, the same impeccable country-house style runs effortlessly throughout: Irish linen, hot-water bottles and Carnegie tartan blankets; beds are turned down each evening. The four-poster is so big it had to be built in its room, there are crystal glasses and decanters in the bedrooms, elegant sofas at the end of beds and seven rooms have open fires. Beautiful antique wardrobes and dressers, fresh flowers, oils, busts, Scottish prints, marble plinths, bowls of fruit – nothing but the best. Bags are carried up to rooms, newspapers come with breakfast – this you can take in your room if you wish. Rooms are large, some are huge, and those at the top of the house have views over chimney pots. You can even play croquet in the gardens across the road, and each evening guests gather for a glass of champagne in the drawing room. Luxurious country-house living in the middle of the city. Wonderful.

Rooms: 11: 5 twin/doubles, 2 doubles, 3 junior suites and 1 four-poster.
Price: £190-£270; suites £320; singles from £190.
Meals: Full breakfast £11.95-£16.95. Room service.
Closed: Christmas.

Tube: Sloane Square.
Bus: 11, 19, 22, 137, 211, C1.
Parking: Nearest car park £25 per 24 hrs.

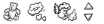

Map: 5

4 First Street

Chelsea
London SW3 2LD

Tel: 020 7581 8429
Fax: 020 7854 0782

Shirley Eaton

I can already hear you thanking me for this one. Not only is this a wonderful house in a highly desirable part of central London, but it is also run by one of the nicest people you are likely to meet in this city, so it's ten out of ten on all counts. Shirley knows her B&B (she works for a rival guide, quite scurrilous!) and her house is warmly welcoming, a perfect home-from-home. You breakfast in the basement by an open fire; you can catch the sun on the pretty decked terrace, pots and olive trees around you; and best of all is the bedroom: big, bright and luxurious – a great place to laze around. You're up at the top of the house, thus nicely private, there's lots of space, it's beautifully decorated and one wall is made of glass that opens onto a tiny balcony. The bathroom is marbled, with a deep bath to soak in and big mirrors – all very indulging. Outside, much locally to attract you. This is shop-till-you-drop land: Walton Street, South Kensington, Sloane Street and King's Road, so take your pick. Four great pubs within a two-minute walk and don't miss La Brasserie for supper.

Rooms: 1 double.
Price: £95-£105; singles £65.
Meals: Continental breakfast included.
Closed: Occasionally.

Tube: Sloane Square;
Knightsbridge;
South Kensington.
Bus: 14, 19, 22, 137.
Parking: Nearest car park £25 per 24 hrs.

Map: 5

Searcy's Roof Garden Bedrooms

30 Pavilion Road
Knightsbridge
London SW1X OHJ

Tel: 020 7584 4921
Fax: 020 7823 8694
E-mail: rgr@searcys.co.uk
Web: www.searcys.co.uk

Alexandra Saric

Only in England could you find a gem like this. Searcy's is a one-off; unique and intimate, a fine Knightsbridge pied-à-terre. From the street you enter directly into a 1927 freight elevator. ("It is forbidden for housemaids to travel alone in the lift with a footman", reads the original sign.) You then ascend three floors, bypassing the 160-year-old catering company of the same name, and enter the roof garden rooms. These have been here since the mid-1960s, grand enough to ignore passing fashions, their sense of solid tradition almost aristocratic. Not that you should take this to be a euphemism for 'faded'. On the contrary, the rooms are delightful: pretty fabrics and wallpaper giving a county-house feel, and there are canopied beds, fresh flowers, a smattering of antiques and quirky bathrooms (with the odd bath actually in the bedroom). Breakfast is brought to you and accompanied occasionally by the sound of the Household Cavalry passing below. Exceptional value so close to Harrods. Hyde Park is a short walk and there's a rooftop terrace where you can relax at the end of the day.

Rooms: 10: 4 doubles, 3 twins, 2 singles and 1 suite.
Price: £130-£170; singles £90-£120.
Meals: Continental breakfast included.
Closed: Christmas and New Year.

Tube: Knightsbridge.
Bus: 9, 10, 14, 19, 22, 52, 74, 137.
Parking: Nearest car park £25 per 24 hrs.

Map: 5

Parkes Hotel

41 Beaufort Gardens
Knightsbridge
London SW3 1PW

Tel: 020 7581 9944
Fax: 020 7581 1999
E-mail: info@parkeshotel.com
Web: www.parkeshotel.com

Susan Burns

A top-to-bottom refurbishment, an entire renovation, a cool three million lavished on this lap of luxury, and the result: perfection down to the tiniest detail. In the Italian-marble bathrooms you get heated floors and mirrors, shower heads the size of cymbals, deep cast-iron baths and mountains of towels. Bedrooms are no less indulging: huge rooms, high ceilings, sleigh beds, bowls of fruit, modem points, DVD players, stunning fabrics, glistening chandeliers, and 18 different malts in the mini-bar. Nothing disappoints, least of all the service. Mention the fact there are no plasma screen TVs and you are met with a cast-iron assurance that they'll be here very soon. There are rich Georgian colours on the walls, reds and yellows, greens and clarets; air conditioning in every room, sofas or armchairs, too. If you're thinking of opening a hotel and you'd like to see how it should be done, then this is the place for you. Alternatively, just come and enjoy. Harrods is a one-minute walk from this peaceful, tree-lined square.

Rooms: 32: 4 singles, 9 doubles,
2 twins, 3 junior suites and 14 suites.
Price: £280-£340; junior suites £380;
suites £490; singles £230.
Weekend rates available.
Meals: Full breakfast £5 in breakfast room
or £10 in your bedroom.
Closed: Never.

Tube: Knightsbridge.
Bus: 14, 74, C1.
Parking: Nearest car park £25 per 24 hrs.

Map: 5

The Beaufort

33 Beaufort Gardens
Knightsbridge
London SW3 1PP

Tel: 020 7584 5252
Fax: 020 7589 2834
E-mail: info@thebeaufort.co.uk
Web: www.thebeaufort.co.uk

James Smith

Two minutes from Harrods (they should hold an annual race, first one to get to haberdashery), but even diehard shopaholics may linger just a little longer in their luxurious rooms. This was the first private house-hotel to open in London and it still has the feel of a home-from-home, albeit quite a grand one. No reception, a complimentary bar, a huge bowl of red apples by the front door and flowers everywhere. Porters swoop and carry bags upstairs to fabulous rooms. These are large, the doubles not much smaller than the suites, and if you imagine all the little (and big) extras you'd like to find in a room – well, they're here: fresh flowers, marble bathrooms, towelling bathrobes, bowls of fruit, the best linen, plush fabrics, CD players, TVs, air conditioning, modem points... if they haven't got it and you need it, they'll do their best to find it for you. Breakfast is brought to your room, the Wedgwood china resting on starched linen tablecloths. A relaxing, spoiling place, with thoughtful, dedicated staff who give the place a very friendly feel. It's in a cul-de-sac, so there's hardly any noise.

Rooms: 28: 18 twin/doubles, 7 suites and 3 singles.
Price: £180-£280; singles from £155; suites from £295.
Meals: Continental breakfast included.
Closed: Never.

Tube: Knightsbridge.
Bus: 14, 74, C1.
Parking: Harrods car park £25 per 24 hrs.

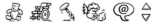

Map: 5

37 Trevor Square

Knightsbridge
London SW7 1DY

Tel: 020 7823 8186
Fax: 020 7823 9801
E-mail: margaret@37trevorsquare.co.uk
Web: www.37trevorsquare.co.uk

Margaret & Holly Palmer

A fabulous find, luxury in the middle of Knightsbridge, the sort of thing for which hotels would charge a fortune. Trevor Square is incredibly pretty, unexpectedly peaceful and only a three-minute walk from Hyde Park or Harrods. Margaret and Holly are a mother-and-daughter team who run an interior design company, rather successfully by the look of things. Impeccable furniture and furnishings throughout; in the large bedroom you'll find TV, DVD and CD players, a complimentary bar, an electric blanket, a cashmere duvet and maple tables. You get the whole of the top floor, which includes a hugely luxurious marbled bathroom (big mirrors, deep bath, power shower), and a small sitting room, which has an extra bed if you need it. Margaret does breakfast down in the dining room (you get the full English works, or smoked salmon and scrambled eggs), or you can eat in the tiny courtyard in good weather. There are hundreds of restaurants nearby, one of which, San Lorenzo's, was one of Princess Diana's favourites. And just in case you've forgotten, the Harrods' sales are in January and June.

Rooms: 1 double.
Price: £120; singles £100.
Meals: Full breakfast included.
Closed: Occasionally.

Tube: Knightsbridge.
Bus: 9, 10, 14, 19, 22, 52, 74, 137.
Parking: Nearest car park £25 per 24 hrs (closed overnight).

Map: 5

57 Pont Street

Knightsbridge
London SW1X 0BD

Tel: 020 7590 1090
Fax: 020 7590 1099
E-mail: no57@no57.com
Web: www.no57.com

Laurence Bloom

A grand old London building – red-brick, high ceilings, ornate plaster work – brought into the 21st century with a funky make-over of purples, browns, reds and whites. Number 57 is a minimalist's dream: lots of space, clean lines, no clutter. In reception, a triangle of smooth concrete upon which rests a bowl of red apples, the odd strip of shiny blue neon embedded in a wall and ivory-coloured silk curtains draped over a door. There is a lift to whisk you around, but if you walk down, you pass landings full of mirrored doors, porthole lights, busts on plinths and more draped silk. Contemporary bedrooms have neutral colours on the walls, cedar-wood blinds, smoked-glass wardrobes, and, in most rooms, a piece or two of modern art. Rooms vary in size but even the small are a good size, not cramped at all, and the big are just that, with plasma screen TVs. Charcoal wool blankets, crisp white linen, and in the bathrooms, mosaic tiles in blues, greens or reds. Back downstairs, cherry-red walls in a warm and stylish bar/sitting room, with brown cord sofas, slick wooden tables and an open fire. Very central.

Rooms: 21: 11 doubles, 4 twins, 1 single and 5 studios.
Price: £205-£295; singles from £145. Weekend rates available.
Meals: Continental breakfast £10. Room service.
Closed: Never.

Tube: Knightsbridge; Sloane Square.
Bus: 19, 22, 137.
Parking: Nearest car park £25 per 24 hrs.

  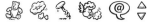 **Map: 5**

L'Hotel

28 Basil Street
Knightsbridge
London SW3 1AS

Tel: 020 7589 6286
Fax: 020 7823 7826
E-mail: reservations@lhotel.co.uk
Web: www.lhotel.co.uk

Isabel Murphy

L'Hotel is well-named – it has the feel of a small Parisian hotel, but chief among its many bounties is Isabel, who, in her short reign (long live the Queen), has proved it is not only what you do, but how you do it that matters. Her way is infectious; she is kind and open and nothing is too much trouble. The hotel's not bad either. Downstairs there's a great little restaurant/bar for breakfast, lunch and dinner – the social hub of the place – where the odd note of jazz rings out. You can have breakfast down here – excellent coffee in big bowls, pains au chocolat, croissants – or they'll happily deliver it to your room where you can laze about on vast beds that are covered in Egyptian cotton, with Nina Campbell fabric on the walls, little box trees on the mantlepiece, original art on the walls and an occasional open fireplace. Turn left on your way out and Harvey Nicks is a hundred paces; turn right and Harrods is closer. If you want to eat somewhere fancy, try the Capital next door. It has a big reputation, is owned by the same family, and Isabel will book you in. A very friendly, very pretty place.

Rooms: 12: 11 twin/doubles and 1 suite.
Price: £165-£175; suite from £190.
Meals: Continental breakfast included, full English from £6.
Lunch & dinner £6-£15.
Closed: Never.

Tube: Knightsbridge.
Bus: 14, 19, 22, 52, 74, 137, C1.
Parking: £25 a day off-street.

Map: 5

Basil Street Hotel

8 Basil Street
Knightsbridge
London SW3 1AH

Tel: 020 7581 3311
Fax: 020 7581 3693
E-mail: info@thebasil.com
Web: www.thebasil.com

Charles Lagares

The Basil does not follow fads and fashions, it is far too English for that. It is a throwback to the days of Empire, a place one might expect to find in India rather than in SW3. It is where diplomats gather for tea and where the Major-General holds the regimental dinner. The Gallery walkway is modelled on that of an old P&O liner, with writing desks in alcoves and a parliamentary clock upon the wall. At supper, dine on lobster bisque and roast rib of Scottish beef while the pianist plays gentle melodies from the past and the waiter asks, "will you have the bread and butter pudding, sir?" Run by eccentrics for eccentrics, this is the hotel that people who hate hotels adore. It is spread over six luxurious floors, though you should not expect to land on the first floor if you press '1' in the lift; that would be too easy. Bedrooms, which vary in size but not style, are liberally sprinkled with antiques, as is the rest of the hotel. You'll find Delft-tiled fireplaces, French *armoires* and Edwardian writing desks. Brilliant.

Rooms: 80: 21 doubles, 22 twins, 4 family, 33 singles.
Price: £235; family rooms £325; singles £165. Weekend rates £210.
Meals: Continental breakfast £11, full English £15. Lunch and dinner £15-£25. Afternoon tea £12.50. Room service.
Closed: Never.

Tube: Knightsbridge.
Bus: 9, 10, 14, 19, 22, 52, 74, 137.
Parking: Nearest car park £25 per 24 hrs.

Map: 5

16 William Mews

Knightsbridge
London SW1X 9HF

Tel: 020 7259 6645
Fax: 020 7259 6645
E-mail: marypotter@london01.fsnet.co.uk

Mary Potter

You'll be hard pressed to find better value than this (though that should be a much-repeated refrain in this book). Mary's mews house is in the centre of Knightsbridge; the Beatles once lived in the street, and if you fall out of bed, you land in Harvey Nicks; well, nearly. Incredibly, you get the whole of the basement, the only drawback being pavement lights in the bedroom. But if you don't mind that (and if you're not sure, then you don't), come for peace and quiet in the heart of the city. An easy house to find – it's the one with all the flower pots outside: geraniums, camellias and lavender add their sweep of colour. Only for the nimble: a narrow spiral staircase leads down to your pad. Here you find sitting room, kitchen, bathroom and shower. Japanese prints on the walls, loads of London guides, a tapestry hanging above the bed and a lived-in feel; nothing nasty passed my eagle eye. Breakfast is brought to you. There's a lovely single room upstairs, too, with a faux-marble bathroom, mirrors, flowers, good art – very smart. Hyde Park is a two-minute walk, as are hundreds of restaurants. Mary, who is easy-going, will advise.

Rooms: 2: 1 double, 1 single.
Price: £75-£85; single £55.
Meals: Continental breakfast included.
Closed: Occasionally.

Tube: Knightsbridge.
Bus: 9, 10, 14, 19, 22, 52, 137.
Parking: Nearest car park £25 per 24 hrs.

Map: 5

The Goring

Beeston Place
Victoria
London SW1W 0JW

Tel: 020 7396 9000
Fax: 020 7834 4393
E-mail: reception@goringhotel.co.uk
Web: www.goringhotel.co.uk

George Goring

The Goring is a London institution, an epitome of Englishness, with a dining room for Dover sole or breast of pheasant and a bar for oysters and champagne. Ninety- two years a hotel with a Goring ever at the helm, it is the oldest family-run hotel in London, built in 1910 by O. R. Goring, the first hotel in the world to have central heating and a private bathroom in every room. It is a grand place with its own traditions: George still holds a cocktail party for guests on Sunday evenings. Enter a world of marble floors, yellow walls and glittering chandeliers by the dozen. Liveried doormen at reception dress like Napoleonic generals (their manner more convivial, no doubt); one of them, Peter, has worked here for over 30 years. Good-sized bedrooms are as you'd expect – smart and traditional with a dash of flair: crisp linen, woollen blankets, plush carpets and fresh flowers; bathrooms are wood-panelled. Rooms at the back have garden views. Huge attention to detail throughout the hotel and impeccable service from a devoted staff. Two minutes from Buckingham Palace, yet Beeston Place is remarkably quiet for central London.

Rooms: 74: 47 twin/doubles, 20 singles and 7 suites.
Price: £265-£325; suites from £350; singles £225. Weekend rates available.
Meals: Full breakfast £12.50-£16.50. Lunch £25; dinner £38. Room service.
Closed: Never.

Tube: Victoria.
Bus: 2, 8, 16, 36, 38, 52, 73, 82.
Parking: Private car park £21 per 24 hrs.

The Dorchester

Park Lane
Mayfair
London W1A 2HJ

Tel: 020 7629 8888
Fax: 020 7409 0114
E-mail: reservations@dorchesterhotel.com
Web: www.dorchesterhotel.com

David Wilkinson

Walk in through the revolving doors and you're greeted by a battalion of liveried doormen who glide effortlessly across marble floors, under an ornate gilded ceiling that defies overstatement. Keep going and you're in the Promenade through which all Dorchester life flows – a place to take the famous afternoon tea, indulge in a spot of people-watching, or just schmooze the day away. It's *the* place to linger, stunningly beautiful, terribly grand; a window back in time to an England that once was. Bedrooms are what you'd expect of this sublime hotel: the crispest linen, the plushest fabrics, fabulous marble bathrooms, pure heaven. The Oliver Messel suite is considered one of the finest hotel suites in the world (and comes with a price tag of £2,100 a night), but all rooms elate. Downstairs in the piano bar there's Liberace's mirrored piano, while in the Grill Room you'll eat the best roast beef in the world. I haven't really scratched the surface, but if you're looking for somewhere very special, then this is it. Weekend rates available, so ask when booking. Superb.

Rooms: 250: 170 doubles,
30 twins, 50 suites.
Price: £360-£440; suites from £560;
weekend rates from £315 for two,
breakfast included.
Meals: Continental breakfast £19.50,
full English £23. Lunch and dinner
from £25. Room service.
Closed: Never.

Tube: Green Park.
Bus: 2, 10, 16, 36, 73, 74, 82, 137.
Parking: Brick St car park £35 per 24 hrs.

Map: 2

Athenæum Hotel and Apartments

116 Piccadilly
Mayfair
London W1J 7BJ

Tel: 020 7499 3464
Fax: 020 7493 1860
E-mail: info@athenaeumhotel.com
Web: www.athenaeumhotel.com

Jonathan Critchard

When Margaret Thatcher recently had her house renovated, she moved in here to avoid the builders. The Athenæum stands on Piccadilly, just across the road from Green Park, so you can stroll across to Buckingham Palace and watch the Changing of the Guard. The hotel is grand, yet intimate. In reception there are swathes of fabric, bowls of fruit, liveried doormen (including Donald, something of an institution) and, behind shiny brass doors, a lift waiting to carry you up to fine rooms. Typically, these pile luxury upon luxury: marble bathrooms, heated mirrors (they don't steam up), the best fabrics, hugely comfortable king-size beds, TVs, CDs, videos, and lots of space. If you want added privacy, take a country-house-style apartment (just as luxurious, but bigger and with private entrance). Each has a sitting room and kitchen, too. There's a snug bar just off reception, well-stocked with 230 malts, a sofa-strewn sitting room at the back, and a bright and stylish dining room. If you want to eat out walk round the corner to Shepherd's Market for great restaurants.

Rooms: 156: 110 twins, doubles and singles; 12 suites; 34 one-bedroom apts.
Price: £335-£400; suites and apartments from £490. Weekend rates from £199 for two, breakfast included.
Meals: Continental breakfast £14.50, full English £18.50. Lunch and dinner from £15. Room service.
Closed: Never.

Tube: Green Park.
Bus: 8, 9, 14, 19, 22, 38.
Parking: Brick St car park £35 per 24 hrs.

Map: 2

The Stafford

16-18 St James's Place
St. James's
London SW1A 1NJ

Tel: 020 7493 0111
Fax: 020 7493 7121
E-mail: info@thestaffordhotel.co.uk
Web: www.thestaffordhotel.co.uk

Terry Holmes

The union flag flies outside the Stafford, which stands a mere 12 paces from Green Park and a three-minute stroll from Buckingham Palace. Clarence House, too, is on your doorstep; this is the epicentre of Royal St James's. In the American bar – voted 'Best Hotel Bar in the World' by Forbes magazine – flags, caps, pictures and general memorabilia of past guests tell the hotel's story; some of it would fetch a king's ransom at auction. A very private place, where you should expect a level of luxury and service that is rare in London; this is one of the capital's loveliest hotels. It's also blissfully quiet, its position in a cul-de-sac soundproofing it from the roar of the city. The Carriage House rooms in the cobbled courtyard at the back date from 1650. They were once the stables of Lord Godolphin and the beams in the first-floor rooms are reclaimed ship's timbers from pre-Nelson days. Marble bathrooms, antique furnishings, fabulous artwork, and every single minute extra you could possibly think of. The private dining room in the wine cellars (Terry will give you a tour) is candlelit at night, and must be one of London's finest.

Rooms: 81: Mix of doubles, singles, four-posters, suites and Carriage House rooms.
Price: £260-£365; suites from £425; Carriage House rooms from £430; singles £260.
Meals: Continental breakfast £14.50, full English £16.50. Lunch and dinner from £25. Room service.
Closed: Never.

Tube: Green Park.
Bus: 9, 14, 19, 22, 38.
Parking: Nearest car park £25 per 24 hrs.

Map: 2

22 Jermyn Street

St. James's
London SW1Y 6HL

Tel: 020 7734 2353
Fax: 020 7734 0750
E-mail: office@22jermyn.com
Web: www.22jermyn.com

Laurie Smith

If you stick a pin into the middle of a map of London, it will land in Jermyn Street. It is a quintessential London street, where a gentleman comes to buy his double-cuffed shirts from Harvie & Hudson, then have his whiskers trimmed at the barber's. And he will stay at Number 22, in the luxury to which he has become accustomed. A perfect London base that does nothing but spoil you: roses in marble bathrooms, sofas to sink into, regal fabrics, crisp white linen, dramatic flowers erupting from glass vases. There are antique tables and writing desks, bowls of tangerines and walnuts. Cushions are plumped up by the chambermaids to a prescribed level, then the housekeeper comes in with her ruler to check! Staff are impeccable, kind and courteous; nothing is too much trouble. Go out at night for supper (try Rowley's across the road) and return to find your bed turned down; wake up in the morning and your breakfast will be brought to your room. Five minutes by foot from the front door and you find art galleries, royal palaces, government buildings, West End theatres, parks... and Fortnum & Mason for tea.

Rooms: 18: 5 doubles and 13 suites.
Price: £245; suites £345-£410.
Meals: Full breakfast from £12.65.
Room service.
Closed: Never.

Tube: Piccadilly.
Bus: 8, 9, 14, 19, 22, 38
Parking: Nearest car park £30 per 24 hrs.

Map: 2

North Central

Marble Arch
Paddington
Little Venice
Marylebone
Bond Street
Bedford Square
Bloomsbury
Russell Square

Little Venice

But now behold,
In the quick forge and working-houses of thought,
How London doth pour out her citizens.

William Shakespeare, 'Henry V'

Hyde Park Garden Mews

Marble Arch
London W2

Tel: 020 7351 3445
Fax: 020 7351 9383
E-mail: inquiries@uptownres.co.uk

An 1840s cobbled mews through which horses clop on their way to the Hyde Park circuit. Sue is lovely, a magistrate and very easy to talk to: don't feel you have to remain in your room. You enter directly into her pretty, yellow-and-coral sitting room, with Russell Flint prints on the wall and family pictures everywhere. The place is open-plan: sitting room, kitchen and dining room all merge seamlessly, and you breakfast with the newspaper at an oval mahogany table. Upstairs, two bedrooms, both singles – something of a find for single people, though rooms are only let to the same party, so if he snores too loudly… Both rooms are attractive and homely, a good size and with plenty of storage space. There are books to divert you, woollen blankets to warm you and, one step across the landing, a small but gorgeous bathroom in pastel greens and yellows. No noise at night – mews houses are generally quiet. Hyde Park is a short walk and you're close to Speaker's Corner, so stroll up on a Sunday morning for a dose of controlled madness. Nearby, there are two good locals, the Victoria and the Archer; both do good food, too.

Rooms: 2 singles sharing bathroom (same-party bookings only).
Price: £65-£75 p.p.
Meals: Continental breakfast included.
Closed: Occasionally.

Tube: Marble Arch.
Bus: 12, 16, 74, 94.
Parking: Connaught St car park £25 per 24 hrs.

Map: 2

Norfolk Crescent

Paddington
London W2

Tel: 020 7351 3445
Fax: 020 7351 9383
E-mail: inquiries@uptownres.co.uk

Your hostess Micee effervesces. I caught her a couple of weeks after she had moved house and she was marshalling a bevy of devoted builders, plumbers and decorators into doing the impossible: transforming her new home at record speed. This is all the more incredible when you consider her style: wonderfully rich gold curtains tumble from ceilings, gilt-framed mirrors grace the walls, ornate French writing desks or cabinets inlaid with shining brass fill the rooms; gold is Micee's favourite colour. And she clearly doesn't do 'small'. She bought the house because of the size of the bedrooms; they are gigantic. Crowns sweep down from above big beds, ivory-coloured sofas rest against the walls. There are thick padded headboards, flowers everywhere, glass-topped bedside tables and good lighting. The room at the front has views of Norfolk Crescent, where baskets of flowers hang from traditional lamp posts. You're central, close to Paddington for the Heathrow Express, and there are hundreds of restaurants on your doorstep; try the Beirut Express on Edgware Road for fantastic kebabs.

Rooms: 3: 1 double; 1 twin;
1 twin/double.
Price: £85-£95; singles from £65.
Meals: Continental breakfast included.
Closed: Occasionally.

Tube: Marble Arch;
Paddington;
Edgware Road.
Bus: 6, 7, 15, 16, 23, 27, 36, 98.
Parking: Nearest car park £25 per 24 hrs.

The Colonnade, The Little Venice Town House

2 Warrington Crescent
Little Venice
London W9 1ER

Tel: 020 7286 1052
Fax: 020 7286 1057
E-mail: res_colonnade@etontownhouse.com
Web: www.etontownhouse.com

Oliver Brown

Alan Turing, the Enigma code breaker, was born here, Sigmund Freud visited in 1938, and in the JFK suite you sleep in a four-poster bed made for the man himself. The Colonnade is grand and gracious, decidedly English, with strong echoes of the past, the sort of place you read about in Graham Greene novels. There are high ceilings, huge windows, ornate fireplaces, and Doric columns stand sentry outside. The interior is a perfect fusion of classical and contemporary styles, with colour and warmth the defining features: rich reds, glowing golds and deep greens all feature; those who like their hotels in various hues of grey should not apply. Impeccable staff create a relaxed atmosphere, and a full turn-down service pampers: curtains are drawn, lights turned on and *Time Out* opened to the day's telly. Rooms come with crushed velvet blankets, Egyptian cotton bedlinen, bathrobes to pad about in, bowls of apples; a couple also have balconies. A glass-ceilinged restaurant is on the way, and in summer you can eat in the garden. The idyllic canals of Little Venice are a three-minute stroll. There's Mouse, the house cat, too.

Rooms: 43: 26 doubles, 9 singles and 8 suites.
Price: £148-£210; suites £260-£295.
Meals: Full breakfast included. Lunch and dinner, £5-£25. Room service.
Closed: Never.

Tube: Warwick Road.
Bus: 6, 46, 187.
Parking: Nearest car park £20 per 24 hrs.

Map: 1

22 York Street

Marylebone
London W1U 6PH

Tel: 020 7224 2990/3990
Fax: 020 7224 1990
E-mail: mc@22yorkstreet.prestel.co.uk
Web: www.myrtle-cottage.co.uk/callis.htm

Michael & Liz Callis

The Callis family live in two 1820s, Georgian-style town houses in W1, not your average London residence and one that defies all attempts to pigeonhole it. There may be 18 bedrooms, but you should still expect the feel of home: Michael is determined to keep things friendly and easy-going. This might explain the salsa dancing lessons that once broke out at breakfast, a meal of great conviviality taken communally around a curved wooden table in the big and bright kitchen/dining room. Here, a weeping ficus tree stands next to the piano, which, of course, you are welcome to play. There's always something to catch your eye, be it the red-lipped oil painting outside the dining room or the old boots on the landing. Wooden floors run throughout, and each house has a huge sitting room (original high ceilings and shuttered windows), one with a grand piano, the other with sofas, books and backgammon. Expect silk eiderdowns, good beds and lots of space in the bedrooms: all are spotless and very comfortable. Madame Tussaud's, Regent's Park and Lord's are all close by, as are hundreds of restaurants. A very friendly place.

Rooms: 18: A mix of twins, doubles, family and single rooms, 3 with private bathroom, the rest with bathroom or shower.
Price: £100-£115; singles from £82.50.
Meals: Continental breakfast included.
Closed: Never.

Tube: Baker Street.
Bus: 2, 13, 30, 74, 82, 113, 139, 274.
Parking: Chiltern St car park £23 per 24 hrs.

Map: 2

Number Ten

10 Manchester Street
Marylebone
London W1U 4DG

Tel: 020 7486 6669
Fax: 020 7224 0348
E-mail: stay@10manchesterstreet.fsnet.co.uk
Web: www.10manchesterstreet.com

Neville Isaac

In a city where a good night's sleep in a hotel can cost a fortune, Number Ten has good rooms without frills at reasonable prices. The smaller doubles here cost £120 a night, which, given that you're only a five-minute walk from Oxford Street, is good value indeed. Rooms are simple and spotless, with good use of space and natural colours, comfortable beds and crisp linen. Bathrooms are fine, too, and you also get TVs, mini hi-fis, a box of chocolates – and fans, in case we get a summer. Bay trees stand guard outside this 1919 red-brick building, while staff wait to usher you into the lift and to carry your bags up to your room. There's a smart colonial feel to the sitting room with seagrass matting, bamboo blinds and big sofas; then, downstairs, a basement breakfast room. No restaurant, but you are given a London-wide restaurant guide and the best advice on the local hotspots. Theatre tickets can be booked, taxis called. The Wallace Collection, which has re-opened after years of magnificent restoration, is at the end of the road; don't miss it.

Rooms: 46: 18 doubles, 19 twins and 9 suites.
Price: £120-£170; singles from £95; suites £195.
Meals: Continental breakfast included, full English £5.
Closed: Never.

Tube: Bond Street; Baker Street.
Bus: 2, 10, 23, 94, 137.
Parking: Chiltern St car park £23 per 24 hrs.

23 Greengarden House

St. Christopher's Place
Bond Street
London W1U 1NL

Tel: 020 7935 9191
Fax: 020 7935 8858
E-mail: info@greengardenhouse.com
Web: www.greengardenhouse.com

Nikki Pybus

Under Nikki's expert eye all things run smoothly at Greengarden House. These serviced apartments on pedestrianised St Christopher's Place are a stone's throw from Oxford Street and Bond Street tubes, yet you get loads of space, lots of style, and peace and quiet in the city. You can choose between a contemporary design (slick Italian furniture, glass tables, neutral colours, airy rooms, huge sofas), or a more antiquey, country-house look (plush fabrics, good wooden furniture, padded headboards, bolder colours). All are lovely, the idea here being to provide both style and substance in a central London base. Thus, you get the TVs and videos in the sitting room, a hi-tech kitchen, an overdose of luxury in the bathroom, and a weekday maid service to keep it all clean. You also get your own phone (and phone number) and a modem point. If you need something done, Nikki will see to it: food shopping, babysitting, car hire, theatre tickets – just whatever you want; the service here is impeccable. A very pretty part of London, with a thriving restaurant district on your doorstep. And a few shops, too!

Rooms: 23: 15 one-bedroom apartments; 8 two-bedroom apartments.
Price: One-bedroom apts. £220-£260; two-bedroom apts. £295-£360.
Meals: Full kitchen facilities for guests.
Closed: Never.

Tube: Bond Street.
Bus: 2, 10, 12, 74, 137, 159.
Parking: Nearest car park £33 per 24 hrs.

Map: 2

myhotel Bloomsbury

11-13 Bayley Street
Bedford Square
London WC1B 3HD

Tel: 020 7667 6000
Fax: 020 7667 6001
E-mail: guest_services@myhotels.co.uk
Web: www.myhotels.co.uk

Tanja Koch

An ultra-minimalist fantasy hotel of eastern inspiration, a popular haunt with media types. Conran designed the interiors, then in came a feng shui expert, who moved all the mirrors around to keep the karma cool. Leather sofas, stone floors, and tropical fish swimming in a wall of glass in reception, while downstairs in the basement you can indulge in a bit of *Jinja* – ancient eastern treatments to refresh your body; the more orthodox can work out in a gym. After which you will need sustenance: try either mybar – leather benches, wooden floors, modern art – for light Mediterranean-style food, or cross the hall to Yo!Sushi for quick, cool Japanese dishes that you pluck from the passing conveyer belt. Expect a level of service you rarely find in a hotel, with staff primed to deal with your most trifling needs 24 hours a day; just pick up the phone and ask. Bedrooms are excellent, uncluttered, of course, with halogen lighting, Conran sofas, neutral colours, waffle blankets, mosaic-tiled bathrooms, and all the gadgets you'd expect. The apartments at the top are wild – James Bond meets the Dalai Lama; each one has a rooftop garden.

Rooms: 78: a mix of singles, doubles, twins, suites and apartments.
Price: £220-£300; suites from £380; apartments from £530; singles from £175.
Meals: Full breakfast £12-£16.
Room service.
Closed: Never.

Tube: Tottenham Court Road.
Bus: 10, 24, 29, 73, 134.
Parking: Nearest car park £25 per 24 hrs.

Map: 2

The Academy, The Bloomsbury Town House

17-21 Gower Street
Bloomsbury
London WC1E 6HG

Tel: 020 7631 4115
Fax: 020 7636 3442
E-mail: res_academy@etontownhouse.com
Web: www.etontownhouse.com

Margaret Kavanagh

There are imitation leopard-skin cushions on the suede sofa, and flowers from the jungle that erupt from enormous vases. Lions and tigers prowl – well, sketches of them hang on the walls, by Degas, Rubens and Rembrandt. It may not sound too 'WC1', but you couldn't be anywhere but England: the old leather armchairs, the roaring fire and the warm glow of yellow-papered Georgian walls are unmistakably English. An immaculate hotel, a real find for those in search of a smart country house in town. The five 1780 houses are linked by labyrinthine corridors: you may need a ball of string; but if you fear getting lost, just hole up in the splendour of your room. You'll find plump pillows on wooden beds, Egyptian cotton bedlinen, exposed marble fireplaces, the odd free-standing bath, country-chic fabrics, bold colours, fresh flowers and bowls of apples. Bigger rooms are just that; all rooms have the same comfort and flair. Downstairs, a conservatory-sitting room leads out to a walled garden with a small fountain, perfect for summer sundowners. Peace and quiet in the city, with Covent Garden and Soho on your doorstep.

Rooms: 49: 21 doubles, 5 twin, 12 singles and 11 suites.
Price: £160-£220; suites £250-£265. Weekend rates available.
Meals: Full breakfast included. Room service.
Closed: Never.

Tube: Tottenham Court Rd; Russell Square; Euston Square.
Bus: 10, 24, 29, 73, 134.
Parking: Private car park £20 per 24 hrs.

Map: 2

University College London

Campbell House
5-10 Taviton Street
Bloomsbury
London WC1H OBX

Tel: 020 7679 1479
Fax: 020 7388 0060
E-mail: accommodation@ucl.ac.uk

Residence Manager

A pioneering seat of learning, "the Godless institution of Gower Street" was founded by "an association of liberals" who took as their model the universities of Germany and Scotland and not the Church of England universities of Oxford and Cambridge. Thus, in 1828, education was made available to men regardless of their religion, and in 1878, to women. Fittingly, these halls of residence were once the home of Hugh Price Hughes, the Methodist preacher, who used to speak from one of the balconies. In summer you can stay for next to nothing. Rooms are basic: clean and tidy, with single beds, easy chairs, wardrobes and chests of drawers, and each corridor has a shared shower block – if you are looking for something cheap and cheerful close to the centre of town, you'll be hard pressed to find better. Breakfast is not included, but there are kitchens where you can store and prepare food, or you can eat out locally. Finally, the "auto-iconic" body of the philosopher Jeremy Bentham remains in the university's South Cloister – they used to bring him out for certain suppers! Ask nicely and they may let you see him.

Rooms: 100: 40 twins, 60 singles; shower blocks shared on each corridor.
Price: £35-£40; singles £18-£22.
Meals: Kitchens available for self-catering.
Closed: Open mid-June to mid-September only.

Tube: Euston.
Bus: 59, 68, 91, 168.
Parking: Nearest car park £25 per 24 hrs.

The Jenkins Hotel

45 Cartwright Gardens
Russell Square
London WC1H 9EH

Tel: 020 7387 2067
Fax: 020 7383 3139
E-mail: reservations@jenkinshotel.demon.co.uk
Web: www.jenkinshotel.demon.co.uk

Sam Bellingham

David Suchet (aka Hercule Poirot) once stood under the pillared porch of the Jenkins Hotel, and even though the director got his shot, Hercule and his mischievous moustache didn't check in, thus calling into question the power of his little grey cells. Sam's quirky B&B hotel is extraordinary given both its price tag and the gentleness of its staff – this is more the sort of family operation you'd expect to find in France, Italy or Spain. No lift and five floors (so no need for a fitness room), but a cantilevered staircase and the odd sloping floor instead. Bedrooms are spotless and have neat carpets, bright fabrics, padded headboards, sheets and blankets. Most rooms have the equivalent of a ship's shower; compact, but does the job nicely. You'll find the odd antique, TVs, mini bars, even safes, but each room is very different (in size as well as style), so if you have a particular requirement, ask when booking. Don't miss the fabulous North Sea Fish Restaurant in nearby Leigh Street for some of the best fish and chips in the capital. Regent's Park is close, and the British Library a short stroll.

Rooms: 13: 8 twin/doubles,
2 triples and 2 singles;
1 single, private shower.
Price: £85-£90; singles £52-£72.
Meals: Full breakfast included.
Closed: Never.

Tube: Russell Square;
King's Cross;
Euston.
Bus: 59, 68, 91, 168.
Parking: Nearest car park £16 per 24 hrs.

Map: 2

The Generator

Compton Place
37 Tavistock Place
Russell Square
London WC1H 9SD

Louise Duffy

Tel: 020 7388 7666
Fax: 020 7388 7644
E-mail: info@the-generator.co.uk
Web: www.the-generator.co.uk

Blade Runner meets *Lonely Planet* at this central London hostel that's won just about all the awards a hostel can win. A futuristic-film-set feel, with metal sculptures, blue neon light, *Clockwork Orange* wall hangings, and value for money at every turn: breakfast is included, you can get fish and chips for £3, and cocktails in the bar at happy hour (6pm-9pm) are £2.50 a pop. There's a reading room with internet access, video games in one dining area, and a juke box in an 'industrial' bar where everything is metal and the lights all blue. The place can sleep up to 800 people so there's always someone about, and staff are friendly and helpful. You can buy London guides, phone cards, plug adaptors and other useful bits and bobs. Bedrooms are basic: bed, sheets, towel, carpet and sink, but all are clean, and if there are four of you, you can pay as little as £18 a night each and get a room to yourselves; dorm beds cost even less. Even the bathrooms (piping hot water 24 hours a day) have been 'funked up'. A second Generator is about to open in Berlin, maybe a third in Amsterdam. If none of the above puts you off, you'll love it.

Rooms: A mix of twins, triples, quads, 5-bed, 6-bed, 8-bed rooms and one 14-bed dorm, with shower blocks on each floor.
Price: Dorms from £10 p.p.; twin rooms from £25 p.p.
Meals: Full breakfast included. Dinner from £3.
Closed: Never.

Tube: Russell Square.
Bus: 59, 68, 91, 168.
Parking: Nearest car park £25 per 24 hrs.

Map: 2

North London

Hampstead
Primrose Hill
Camden
Highbury
Islington

Hampstead from Parliament Hill

London: a nation, not a city.

Benjamin Disraeli, 'Lothair'

La Gaffe

107-111 Heath Street
Hampstead
London NW3 6SS

Tel: 020 7435 8965
Fax: 020 7794 7592
E-mail: la-gaffe@msn.com
Web: www.lagaffe.co.uk

Lorenzo Stella

Real Italian hospitality and great value at La Gaffe. Bernardo and Androulla Stella opened the restaurant in 1962, adding rooms in 1976. Today it's run with the same ineffable charm by their sons, Lorenzo and Salvatore. The list of celebrities who have eaten here is too long to mention, but spaghetti-western-star Clint Eastwood was a regular in the Sixties. The hotel is made up of five former shepherd's cottages built in 1734, well before Hampstead became such a desirable address. It's the highest point in London and the views from Hampstead Heath (across the road) are wonderful. The village itself is full of terraced cafés, trendy boutiques and charming backstreets (including Church Row, said to be the most beautiful in London). The restaurant has recently been redecorated with murals and faux-Roman walls. Expect good traditional Italian cooking – the Stellas get their oils, cheese and hams from an uncle's farm in Abruzzo. Bedrooms aren't huge, but have pretty floral fabrics. Those at the back look onto a quiet Georgian square and two have steam baths. A family-run gem, popular with the locals. Don't miss the meatballs.

Rooms: 18: 6 doubles, 4 twins, 4 singles, 3 four-posters and 1 family.
Price: £90-£125; singles from £65.
Meals: Continental breakfast included. Lunch and dinner, £5-£25.
Closed: Never.

Tube: Hampstead.
Bus: 46, 268.
Parking: £10 a day on-street.

Map: 1

Hampstead Village Guest House

2 Kemplay Road
Hampstead
London NW3 1SY

Tel: 020 7435 8679
Fax: 020 7794 0254
E-mail: info@HampsteadGuesthouse.com
Web: www.HampsteadGuesthouse.com

Annemarie van der Meer

There's nothing mild about the eccentricity here: beds come out of wardrobes, there are tiny, Heath-Robinson, Victorian brass-piped showers, the Amsterdam Barok Ensemble comes to rehearse, and toasters appear from bushes in the garden on fine days. One room has a hidden basin salvaged from a train, another a four-poster bed that once belonged to a German countess, and which moves on rails so you can lie in the sun without getting out of bed. Annemarie is clearly an Olympic champion when it comes to rummaging around in junk/antique shops. Every room has something 'different,' be it a piano, a collection of old LPs and a record player, or a bath in the middle of the room. In the dining room: a packed dresser, where the odd mug comes with a map of the tube, so you can plan your day while you drink your coffee. Phones in the rooms; you can also rent mobiles while you stay and pay as you go. It's a three-minute walk to Hampstead Heath – make sure you get to Parliament Hill. You can stop for a drink at the Freemasons Arms, or head to Zen or La Giraffe for great food.

Rooms: 9: Mix of twins, doubles, singles and family rooms, some with bath or shower, some with private bath/shower rooms.
Price: £84-£96; singles £48-£70.
Meals: Full breakfast included.
Closed: Never.

Train: Hampstead Heath (North London Line).
Tube: Hampstead.
Bus: 24, 46, 168, 268.
Parking: £10 a day on-street.

Map: 2

North

30 King Henry's Road

Primrose Hill
London NW3 3RP

Tel: 020 7483 2871
Fax: 020 7209 9739
E-mail: mail@caroleingram.com
Web: www.30kinghenrysroad.co.uk

Andrew & Carole Ingram

When it comes to writing the definitive book on London B&Bs, Carole will get a chapter of her own. And rightly so; no one has done more to get great London B&Bs up and running, encouraging just about everyone she knows with a good house to start (including at least ten in this book). So come and stay and see how it's done. Stripped wooden floors in the grandish entrance hall; big rooms, bright and airy, with high ceilings and a smart family feel. Pots and pans hang in the kitchen, the Aga warms the room. Seagrass runs through the house, and there are walls of books on the landing. In the bedrooms expect brass beds, bathrobes, crisp linen, old mahogany furniture, winged armchairs – a country-house style. The steel and marble kitchen, with open fire in winter, is the place for breakfast: bagels, rolls, croissants, toast, juice, fruit salad and yogurt. Walk in Primrose Hill; Regent's Park is close by, too. You can stroll down Chalk Farm Road to Camden Lock Market, and the restaurants round here are excellent: Odette's is a favourite and Limonia is a Greek place with a big reputation.

Rooms: 2: 1 twin; 1 double,
private bathroom and shower.
Price: £95-£100; singles £80.
Meals: Continental breakfast included.
Closed: Occasionally.

Tube: Chalk Farm.
Bus: 24, 31, 168.
Parking: £8 a day on-street.

Map: 2

78 Albert Street

Camden
London NW1 7NR

Tel: 020 7387 6813
Fax: 020 7387 1704
E-mail: peter@peterbellarchitects.co.uk

Joanna & Peter Bell

We have two houses in Camden, both owned by architects... who work together. Peter's place is immaculate from top to toe, though it takes a bit of time to get through the hall, so good are his holiday pics that hang on the wall. Upstairs is the kitchen, a room of huge style, designed, of course, by Peter, and supplied by Ikea. Look carefully and you'll see how he's lined up the floor tiles with the kitchen units so the lines flow. What you can't see in the picture are: the floor-to-ceiling window through which Camden light streams; the sofa; the wall of books and library steps; the vase of lilies on the kitchen table. Upstairs to the bedrooms: an attractive bunk room for kids (or adults; they're big enough) with a small library of children's books; and the lilac double, a delightful room with two windows looking onto a leafy street and a nice clean style. In between, an electric-green bathroom. Breakfast often comes from the hand of Christina, who helps around the house. This is Camden's most beautiful residential street (1841), and there are loads of great restaurants close by; try Mignon's for the best Lebanese.

Rooms: 2: 1 twin/double, 1 twin
(bunk beds) sharing bathroom.
Price: £90-£110; singles £45.
Meals: Continental breakfast included.
Closed: Never.

Tube: Camden Town.
Bus: C2, 24, 27, 29, 31, 88, 274.
Parking: Nearest car park £9 per 24 hrs.

Map: 2 83

66 Camden Square

Camden
London NW1 9XD

Tel: 020 7485 4622
Fax: 020 4785 4622
E-mail: rodgerdavis@btinternet.com

Sue & Rodger Davis

A Japanese-style house in a London square, made of glass and African teak. This is a real treat for anyone who yearns for a slice of cool, contemporary living. Fabulous use of space and light, with all the little touches you'd expect from a professional: halogen lighting, porthole mirrors in the bathroom and a pyramid of glass on the roof that brightens still further. Rodger and Sue have travelled widely, and much from abroad decorates their home. The minimalist feel throughout is in keeping with the Japanese spirit. African teak (iroko) is everywhere, including the stairs which you climb to find very special bedrooms. These are in Japanese style: paper lanterns, low-slung beds, modern chairs, no clutter. Both rooms have modern, blue-and-red stained glass windows, and the double has two walls of glass. Breakfast downstairs at a big wooden table looking onto a courtyard garden full of life. There's Peckham the parrot, too. Trendy Camden has several markets (Camden Lock is great for clothes), Regent's Park, the Jazz Café or the Round House Theatre. Lots of good gastro pubs, too.

Rooms: 2: 1 double and 1 single sharing bathroom (same-party bookings only).
Price: £80-£90; singles from £40.
Meals: Continental breakfast included.
Closed: Never.

Tube: Camden Town.
Bus: C2, 24, 27, 29, 31, 88, 274.
Parking: Nearest car park £9 per 24 hrs.

4 Highbury Terrace

Highbury
London N5 1UP

Tel: 020 7354 3210

Marion & Donn Barnes

To quote from a letter Marion wrote after we'd met: "Thanks for your visit, sorry we talked so much... the books you left herewith returned... I will get to bed now; a need to meet a breakfast at 4.30am has arisen." Marion and Donn transcend the art of convivial hospitality; nothing is too much trouble, everything is a natural response, and they will think these words of praise just so much pretty hogwash. A house of laughter, of wandering conversations and spontaneous diversions, where books are brought out to check facts while the kettle works overtime. Nothing is done to impress, which is why everything does. Their 1779 home overlooks the peace and quiet of Highbury Fields (a short walk across it takes you to the tube). Inside, the simple décor is warm and homely, and light floods in through myriad Georgian windows, one 14 feet high. Comfy bedrooms, fresh flowers, pretty linen, throws over chairs, the odd piece from Ikea – nothing jars. The top floor has two bedrooms, kitchen, shower and bath, thus perfect for families. For jazz fans, the Vortex (London's grooviest jazz club) is close by. A great find.

Rooms: 3: 2 twins,
both with private bathrooms;
1 single with private shower and wc.
Price: £60-£70; singles from £35.
Meals: Continental breakfast included.
Closed: Occasionally.

Train: Highbury & Islington.
Tube: Highbury & Islington;
Holloway Road.
Bus: 4, 19, 30, 43.
Parking: Free on-street close by.

Map: 2

26 Florence Street

Islington
London N1 2FW

Tel: 020 7359 5293
Fax: 020 7359 5293
E-mail: valerie.rossmore@onmail.co.uk

Valerie Rossmore

I am under strict orders to mention the theatres around here, especially the Almeida, its reputation so strong that Juliette Binoche, Kevin Spacey and Cate Blanchette (to name but a few) have all been drawn to tread its boards. Valerie comes from a theatrical background, a fact apparent after a milli-second in her vibrant home: sparkling cushions, flourishing colour, incense and wall-hangings – the house is packed with pieces from Morroco, Italy, India and beyond. The double is equally stylish with old Irish linen, stencilled window seats, rugs galore, and a sofa covered in throws. There's an extraordinary sitting room which is actually a tropical conservatory – Eden in N1. It's on two levels and the pretty single downstairs gets part of it, a private sitting room/courtyard. Breakfast is upstairs in the Aga-warmed kitchen/dining room. Here, amid more rustic chic, you breakfast on brioche, croissants, juice and yogurt, fruit and coffee. Masses of shops on your trendy Islington doorstep, and you can eat in the restaurant where Tony and Gordon carved up New Labour.

Rooms: 2: 1 double and 1 single sharing shower.
Price: £85-£95; singles £55.
Meals: Continental breakfast included.
Closed: Rarely.

Tube: Angel; Highbury & Islington.
Bus: 4, 19, 38, 73.
Parking: Nearest car park £25 per 24 hrs.

Map: 2

www.specialplacestostay.com

Adrift on the unfathomable and often unnavigable sea of accommodation pages on the internet, those who have discovered www.specialplacestostay.com have found it to be an island of reliability. Not only will you find a database full of honest, trustworthy, up-to-date information about over a thousand special places to stay across Europe, but also:

- **Direct links to the web sites of hundreds of places from the series**
- **Colourful, clickable, interactive maps**
- **The facility to make most bookings by e-mail –
  even if you don't have e-mail yourself**
- **Online purchasing of our books, securely and cheaply**
- **Regular, exclusive special offers on books from the whole series**
- **The latest news about future editions, new titles and new places**
- **The chance to participate in the evolution of both the guides
  and the site**

The site is constantly evolving and is frequently updated. We're expanding our European maps, adding more useful and interesting links, providing news, updates and special features that won't appear anywhere else but in our window on the world wide web.

Just as with our printed guides, your feedback counts, so when you've surfed all this and you still want more, let us know – this site has been planted with room to grow!

Russell Wilkinson, Web Editor
editor@specialplacestostay.com

Making the most of London

Tourist information in London

There is only one place worth visiting in London for good, impartial tourist advice. It is the **Britain Visitor Centre** at 1 Lower Regent Street, London SW1 (www.visitbritain.com): open 9am-6.30pm Monday to Friday, 10am-4pm weekends. Staff here are friendly and informative, and their bookshop has the largest collection of London guides and maps that I have come across (though the bigger London bookshops should be well-stocked, too). I find the following guides all excellent: *Time Out London, Lonely Planet* and *Footprint's London Handbook*. Staff in hotels often have up-to-date information on what's good and what's not; if you're staying in a B&B, ask your hosts about places to visit – they're Londoners, they will know.

Newspapers and magazines

The Evening Standard is London's newspaper. You can buy it anywhere from about 10.30am. Its web site is www.thisislondon.co.uk. *Metro* is a free paper that you pick up at tube stations. It has cinema listings etc, but it's popular, so pick one up early. *Time Out* is the magazine dedicated to London leisure; whatever you want, start looking here. It has listings for clubs, theatres, cinemas, lectures, concerts, sport etc. You can buy it anywhere or see www.timeout.com. If you want to buy something second-hand in London, try the newspaper *Loot*. It's printed five times a week and you can track down just about anything in its (sometimes bizarre) pages.

Cinemas

London has some excellent independent cinemas. Best of the lot is the **National Film Theatre** (020 7928 3232), "a force of knowledge for anyone who cares about film", to quote Robert Altman. Its three screens are dedicated to world cinema and can be found at South Bank, SE1. It also hosts the London Film Festival for three weeks each November. **Riverside Studios** (020 8237 1111) in Crisp Road, W6 has a good programme of world cinema, both past and present, with double bills daily for only £5.50. Smokers should head to the **Notting Hill Coronet**, the only cinema in which you can smoke in London. The **Odeon Leicester Square** is expensive at £9.50/£10 a ticket, but it has a huge screen and is the venue of most London premieres. There are about 50 cinemas in central London and its immediate fringe. The *Evening Standard* lists them all daily.

Making the most of London

Theatres

The **Donmar** (020 7369 1732) in Covent Garden is the best-known venue for modern English theatre. Sam Mendes (of *American Beauty*-fame) put the place on the map with Nicole Kidman in *The Blue Room*. The **Almeida** (020 7359 4404) in Islington has also been in the vanguard over the last ten years. The **National Theatre** (020 7452 3000) at South Bank, Waterloo, is still a vital force 26 years after its creation. The Royal Shakespeare Company (RSC) remains the guardian of the old boy's work, but embraces modern stuff, too. You can see them at the **Barbican** (020 7638 8891), the **Young Vic** in Waterloo (020 7928 6363), or the **Globe Theatre** (020 7401 9919) at Bankside between May and September (it's open air). The **Royal Court** (020 7565 5000) in Sloane Square also has a good reputation. All listings, including the West End, appear in *The Evening Standard* every day. To book, either contact each theatre direct or try **Ticketmaster** (020 7344 4444 or www.ticketmaster.co.uk).

Museums

Public museums are free, though you may have to pay to see certain temporary or visiting exhibitions. The **Museum of London** (140 London Wall, EC2: 020 7600 3699) charts London's rise from prehistoric times to the present day, via the Romans, the Great Fire and two World Wars. The Cromwell Road/Exhibition Road axis finds London's 'big three': the **Natural History Museum** (020 7942 5000), the **Science Museum** (020 7942 4455) and the **Victoria and Albert** (or V&A: 020 7942 2000). The **British Museum** (Great Russell Street, WC1: 020 7636 1555), Elgin Marbles included, is one of the great museums of the world. The **Design Museum** (28 Shad Thames, SE1: 020 7403 6933; admission £6) is full of cutting-edge innovation. The **MCC Museum at Lord's** (St John's Wood, NW8: 020 7432 1033) has everything for the cricket-obsessed, including the Ashes. The **National Maritime Museum** at Greenwich (SE10: 020 8858 4422; admission £7.50) has all things nautical, including the bullet that killed Nelson;

Making the most of London

you can buy a joint ticket for this and the **Royal Observatory** for under £9.50 and, at the latter, stand on the meridian line. London is also full of small, quirky museums; examples include the **Museum of Gardening History** (Lambeth Palace Road, SE1: 020 7401 8865), the **Petrie Museum of Egyptian Archaeology** (University College London, Malet Place, WC1: 020 7504 2884) and **Thomas Carlyle's House** (24 Cheyne Row, SW3: 020 7352 7087; admission £4), where the writer was visited by friends such as Dickens, Thackeray, Tennyson and Ruskin. For a more detailed list check out www.artgalleries-london.com/museums.

Galleries

London is full of art galleries; many are free but charge for special exhibitions. A selection includes: the **Tate Modern** (Queen's Walk, SE1: 020 7887 8000), the hottest space in town, its huge home in the old Bankside power station as impressive as its content (Picasso, Matisse, Pollock, Mondrian); its sister gallery, **Tate Britain** (Millbank, SW1: 020 7887 8008), is an archive of British art from 1500 onwards; the **Hayward Gallery** (South Bank Centre, SE1: 020 7928 3144; admission about £5) is London's most popular exhibition centre for visiting contemporary shows; the **National Gallery** (Trafalgar Square, WC2: 020 7839 3321) has over 2000 pictures from across the centuries and around the world; the **National Portrait Gallery** (St Martin's Place, WC2: 020 7306 0055) is exactly what it says: portraits of great Brits from the last 500 years or so; the **Queen's Gallery** (Buckingham Gate, SW1: 020 7839 1377) gives partial access to the Royal Collection; the **Royal Academy of Arts** (Piccadilly, W1: 020 7300 8000; admission from £6) is worth a visit for the building alone – a real London gem; the **Whitechapel Art Gallery** (Whitechapel High Street, E1: 020 7522 7888) shows nothing but contemporary art, much of it the work of Young British Artists, as does the **Saatchi Gallery** (98a Boundary Road, NW8: 020 7336 7365; admission £4). For more big names try the **Courtauld Gallery** (Somerset House, Strand, WC2: 020 7848 2526; admission £4) for Van Gogh, Renoir and Monet, or the **Wallace Collection** (Manchester Square, W1: 020 7935 0687) for Titian, Rembrandt and Rubens; finally, the **Dulwich Picture Gallery** (College Road, SE21: 020 8693 5254; admission £3-£5) is the country's oldest public gallery and has a fine collection of old masters. For more listings, check www.artgalleries-london.com: an excellent, in-depth site, which also has an extensive diary page, where you can see what's on each day, week, month – invaluable.

Making the most of London

Music venues
Classical

Four big venues spring to mind, though London is good at classical music on a local level and many churches put on concerts during the year or hold weekly recitals. Of the bigger places, most famous is the **Royal Albert Hall** (Kensington Gore, SW7: 020 7589 8212) which holds its world-renowned Proms concerts from mid-July to mid-September. You can often turn up on the night and get a ticket on the door. The hall itself is one of London's landmark buildings, with the gloriously ornate Albert

Memorial standing in the park opposite. The **South Bank** (SE1: 020 7960 4242) has three spaces for classical music: the **Royal Festival Hall**, the **Queen Elizabeth Hall** and the **Purcell Room** – London's top three, a must for classical-music lovers. The **Barbican** (EC2: 020 7638 8891) holds regular concerts and is the home of the London Symphony Orchestra. **Wigmore Hall** (36 Wigmore Street, W1: 020 7935 2141) is entirely independent and as such has huge variety.

Acoustics, country, folk, Irish...

The **Mean Fiddler** (22-24 High Street, NW10: 020 8691 5490) showcases the best acts: folk-, Irish-, country- and acoustic-music lovers will all be in heaven here; it's worth the journey. The **12 Bar Club** (22-23 Denmark Place, off Denmark Street, WC2: 020 7916 6989) squeezes itself into the smallest of spaces making it London's cosiest night spot; good country, folk and acoustic acts all play here. The **Africa Centre** (38 King Street, WC2: 020 7836 1973) is mostly limited to Friday nights, but good acts play here.

Jazz

Ronnie Scott's (47 Frith Street, W1: 0207439 0747) is London's best-known venue and all the greats come to play. It's not cheap, but very funky. The **Vortex** (139-141 Stoke Newington Church Street, N16: 020 7254 6516) may take some getting to, but this north London crown-jewel of jazz is outstanding and it's where the jazz community gathers;

Making the most of London

an exceptional place. The **Jazz Café** (5 Parkway, NW1: 020 7916 6060) is one of Camden's best-known night spots and popular, too, so book if you want to be sure. **Pizza Express** (10 Dean Street, W1: 020 7437 9595) puts on jazz in the basement seven days a week at 9pm. **606 Club** (90 Lots Road, SW6: 020 7352 5953) in Fulham is firmly established on the London jazz circuit, and opens nightly. Finally, the **Bull's Head** (373 Lonsdale Road, SW13: 020 8876 5241) over in Barnes gets the nod from fanatics and has something every night; good Sunday lunch, too.

Restaurants

I have mentioned restaurants in the text if I know them to be good or if they were heartily recommended by owners. London has thousands of places where you can eat, from workmen's cafés for all-day breakfasts (our real national cuisine) to Gordon Ramsay and his Michelin stars in SW3. Food in London is expensive; the bill never seems to be less than £20 per head, often for no more than a main course and a glass or two of house wine. B&B owners and hotel staff will always be able to recommend somewhere to eat, but if you'd like a more comprehensive source, Harden's publish two excellent guides: *London Restaurants*, and *Good Cheap Eats in London*. You can get them in any London bookshop – your stomach will thank you for it if you do – or see www.hardens.com.

Cafés

Café culture has come to London, but mainly with the big chains, and the British remain suspicious about going out at night to a place where they cannot order alcohol. A shame; it would be good to see a return to the coffee houses of the 18th century which "distinguished London from all other cities". There were over 2000 of them in the early 1700s. A few exceptional places can be found. **Troubadour** (265 Old Brompton Road, SW5) stylishly Bohemian, with poetry nights, live music etc, a great spot to

spend a night. **Bar Italia** (22 Frith Street, W1) is still worth the considerable cost of its excellent coffee – there's nowhere quite like it in town to watch life pass by. Staying in Soho, **Maison Bertaux** (28 Greek Street, W1) was established in 1871 and is still going strong – a real institution. **Paul**, bakery and café (29-30 Bedford Street, WC2),

Making the most of London

brings a little Gallic flair to London. Go west to **Lisboa Patisserie** (57 Goldborne Road, W10) close to the north end of Portobello market – a perfect place. On the other side of town, head for the **Brick Lane Bagel Bake** (159 Brick Lane, E1; open 24 hours a day) for what all the food guides call "the best bagel in London".

Pubs

London has thousands of pubs; the best way to find out if you like one is to have a drink in it. The recommendations that follow are entirely subjective, with an emphasis on places that stock good ale and don't play deafening music. Pubs open at 11 o'clock in the morning and close at 11 o'clock at night. Most are open all day, but the odd one may close in the afternoon. Food is often available, usually until about 9.30pm.

West:

The **White Horse** at Parson's Green (SW6) has been revamped, but still has bags of character, good food and fine beer. The riverside pubs at Hammersmith Bridge (Lower and Upper Mall, W6) are hugely popular in summer. The best of the lot is the **Dove**; follow the riverside path to its ancient front door. Cross the river and walk to Barnes Village for the ever-welcoming **Sun** (Church Road, SW13) on Barnes Green. The **Queen's Head** on Brook Green (W6) isn't the greatest pub in the world, but it has the biggest garden of any pub in London, so, again, good in summer. The **Haverlock** (Masbro Road, W14) does excellent food and is a big hit with locals. The **Scarsdale** (Edwardes Square, W8) has a small, but very pretty garden. The **Windsor Castle** (114 Campden Hill Road, W8) is good both in and out, with snug, panelled rooms and a courtyard garden, very English; as is the nearby, and even snugger **Uxbridge** (Uxbridge Road, W8). The **Churchill Arms** (119 Kensington Church Street, W8: 020 7792 1246) is a London institution, dripping in English memorabilia and serving fabulous Thai food in the back room at ridiculously low prices, but you need to book: it gets tremendously busy. The ever-popular Portobello Road in Notting Hill has lots of pubs and bars; stroll along and take your pick, or take to the back streets and find the **Pelican** (All Saints Road, W11), a fully-organic pub and a rather beautiful one at that. Down in Chelsea,

Making the most of London

the **Phene Arms** (Phene Street, SW3) is a real London boozer, with a good garden for summer sundowners. More popular with Chelsea locals is the **Builder's Arms** (13 Britten Street), a posher place altogether, but still a pub at heart. The **Antelope** (Eaton Terrace, SW1), in one of London's smartest residential areas, does good beer and food and is music-free so you don't have to shout.

Central:
The better pubs tend to be away from the centre, but the odd gem remains. The **Coach and Horses** (Greek Street, W1) is legendary for its association with the writer Jeffrey Barnard; you'll either love it or hate it. **French House** (Dean Street, W1) was a 60s-haunt of writers, musicians, painters et al and has stayed true to its Bohemian roots. The **Cork and Bottle** (Cranbourne Street, WC2) is a long-time London favourite near Leicester Square, but gets very busy in the evenings. For MP-spotting try the **Red Lion** (48 Parliament Street, W1). Holborn – the heart of 15th-century  London – has a couple of good spots; the **Cittie of Yorke** (High Holborn, EC1) and the **Jerusalem Tavern** (55 Britton Street, EC1) both have a bit of olde-worlde charm: fires, cubicle-seating, good beer. For something unique try the **Hope and Sir Loin** (94 Cowcross Street, EC1; closed weekends), overlooking Smithfield's (London's meat market); come early, for breakfast: huge meals of meat washed down with pints of beer – it's where the porters knock off after a hard night's work. In the City try the **Black Friar** (174 Queen Victoria Street, EC4), which is shaped like a piece of cheese, or the **Old Cheshire Cheese** which isn't (145 Fleet Street, EC4), one of London's oldest pubs, and it claims Dickens and Johnson among its former drinkers.

South of the River:
Head to the **Prince of Wales** (Cleaver Square, SE11), a perfect pub in a stunning residential square, for one of the best Sunday lunches in town (get there early); great beer, too. Clapham Old Town (SW4) has a triangle of pubs, the **Sun** being the trendiest, the **Prince of Wales** being the most traditional, while half a mile south is the **Windmill on the Common**, an average pub but hugely popular in summer as you can pick up a drink, then head outside.

Making the most of London

North:

The **Dover Castle** (43 Weymouth Mews, W1) is a good bet with loads of atmosphere, nooks and crannies, etc. For weirdness alone try the **Windsor Castle** (29 Crawford Place, W1), a temple to all things royal and where the Handlebar Club meets to talk moustaches. Upper Street in Islington, N1, has masses of choice – it is the Portobello of the north, just smarter. Try the **Duke of Cambridge** (30 St Peter's Street, N1), another organic pub. The **Engineer** (65 Gloucester Avenue, NW1) has both good food and good beer on the Chalk Farm/Camden border. Lastly, and fittingly so, the **Flask** (14 Flask Walk, NW3) in Hampstead, for old locals, fine beers and a no-compromise traditional feel.

Shopping streets

In the last decade London's shopping has undergone a renaissance. There are more tantalizing little boutiques than ever there were in the Sixties, heaps of delectable delicatessens, and more-beautiful-than-ever flagship stores – if shopping is your passion, then fulfilment is to be found on every corner. This retail heaven promises most, of course, to those with fat wallets, but there are sensuous pleasures in store for the browser too, whether she – or he – be roaming the cavernous acres of the 'top people's store' or dipping into the dusty delights of an antiquarian booksellers on the Charing Cross Road.

Oxford Street to Marylebone
London's most famous, and grid-locked, shopping street, **Oxford Street**, has one saving grace: Selfridges. There's "something for everyone" is Selfridges' motto, and its ten acres house the largest range of lipsticks in Europe – quite apart from exhilarating displays of food and fashion and magical window displays at Christmas. Otherwise Oxford Street is a tidal wave of tourists. Escape the hordes into the pedestrianised refuge of **St Christopher's Place** (essential pit stop: Carluccio's Caffe and shop), then on up to the charmingly old-fashioned **Marylebone High Street**, unlikely home to the chic and the off-beat. Visit Sixty 6 for delicious frocks and retro oddities; the Conran Shop, homeware temple to design; Daunt Books, wonderful for travel; VV Rouleaux, exquisite repository of tassels and trims; and modish Mint, **Wigmore Street**, for *objets*, textiles and glass.

Making the most of London

Bond Street to Piccadilly

Cut south from Oxford Street into **New Bond Street** and **Old Bond Street** (for absolute fabulousness, hard to beat), and stroll down swanky **Burlington Arcade** – with decorum: it's still illegal here to hurry or hum! And on into **Piccadilly** to Fortnum & Mason, London's most stately store. The eau-de-nil-and-gold frontage hints at the grandeur within; the Food Hall is an epicure's paradise. At No. 187 is Hatchards, booksellers by appointment to her Majesty the Queen, elegant, olde-worlde and charming, and behind, **Jermyn Street**, famous for its shirts since 1700.

Regent Street

Up the grand sweep of **Regent Street** to London's most alluring store, Liberty, cherished as much for its 19th-century Arts and Crafts interior (even the lifts are wood-panelled) as for its distinctive 21st-century wares; the oriental rug bazaar is a joy. Tucked away behind Liberty is old Sixties hang-out **Carnaby Street** – a genteel shadow of its former flamboyant self, but still geared towards youth fashion.

Soho

Across to Soho, whose maze of streets is packed with gay bars, late bars, specialist food shops and Berwick Street Market (fruit and veg). Fascinating **Old Compton Street** is home to the Algerian Coffee Stores, founded in 1887, and I Camisa & Son, crammed with olives, oils and wild boar ham. Soho borders the **Charing Cross Road** famous for its bookshops – rambling giant Foyles, and 'lifestyle' bookstore Borders, with coffee shop and comfy chairs – but if commercial booksellers are not your style, pop into Any Amount of Books at No. 62,

a ramshackle antiquarian/second-hand booksellers with masses of charm, and wonderful Zwemmer for books on the arts.

Covent Garden

It's a short stroll from here to Covent Garden. Once London's leading wholesale fruit, veg and flower market, Covent Garden is a tourist magnet that bustles with shops and boutiques, open-air cafés and pavement performers (London's best). Away from the Market Hall and Piazza is a cluster of small streets teeming with independent, quirky shops. Head for **Neal's Yard** for vegan bakes; **Neal Street** for Mango's Spanish fashion, and

Making the most of London

Neal Street East, treasure trove of 'orientalia'; cobbled **Floral Street** for Paul Smith and a shop devoted to Tintin; **Earlham Street** for Kitschen Sync (the kitschest trinkets in town) and the Wild Bunch (amazing flowers).

Notting Hill

Wealthy, bohemian Notting Hill holds incomparable distractions. Away from the thronging crowds of **Portobello** are streets filled with restaurants and shops appealing to an adventurous clientele. For kooky, handmade hats go to Christine Bec, **Westbourne Park Road**; to Aimé, **Ledbury Road**, for a minimalist mix of  candles, ceramics and French fashion; **Blenheim Crescent** for the East West Gallery – modern art in a friendly setting – and Books for Cooks, with its own test kitchen; **Elgin Crescent** for Graham & Green, a trio of boutiques selling stylish clothes, accessories and gifts; and **Westbourne Grove** – the western, covetable end – for Christopher Farr's inspirational rugs, Emma Hope's enchanting shoes and Tom (Conran)'s divine deli.

Holland Park

Neighbouring Holland Park is home to the chicest cul-de-sac in London: **Clarendon Cross**. French, whimsical kitchenware (old and new) from Summerill & Bishop, antique clothes from Virginia, cutting-edge florals (peg-bags and pyjamas) from Cath Kidston, and the *dernier cri* in exquisite things – from camisoles to candles – at The Cross, whose cult followers include Jade Jagger.

Chelsea

The **King's Road** is as vibrant a thoroughfare as it was in its Sixties heyday. Head for Heal's (at 234) or Designer's Guild (267) for characterful home furnishings; the beautiful Sundance Market (250) for all things organic; Rococo (321) for chocolately treats in a glamorous setting; Brora (344) for colourful cashmere and funky knits; Couverture (310) for cocooning nightwear; Steinberg & Tolkein (193) for chic vintage gear.

Knightsbridge

If designer stores are your weakness, **Sloane Street** is your destination. From modish Prada and uber-chic Marni to vivid Versace, this Knightsbridge avenue reeks of class. Queening it at the top end is sleek, streamlined Harvey Nichols, style shrine for the rich and famous. Harrods – a five-minute walk from Harvey Nicks – is inelegant in comparison, but then it is a self-contained empire, and has the most magnificent

Making the most of London

toy department in London (and all on one floor, unlike Hamleys). But beware: decorum dictates you leave your rucksack – and/or ripped jeans – behind. If not, the doormen in the green top hats may send you packing.

Street markets

There are lots all over London, some for clothes, some for fruit and vegetables, and some old traditional meat or fish markets. The following are worth a diversion. **Smithfield**, EC1 is London's meat market, the last of the big markets to survive in its original home. Smithfield (smooth field) has been associated with livestock for nine hundred years; it was originally a place to buy horses. **Billingsgate Fish Market** (Trafalgar Way, E14) is open to the public, but set the alarm clock; it's all over by 8am and at its best around 6am. Other good food markets (fruit and veg) include **Berwick Street**, W1 – well worth a visit – and **Borough** (Borough High Street, SE1: weekends only), for all things edible; it's become a firm London favourite in recent years. For flowers try the much-loved **Columbia Road Market** (Bethnal Green, E2; Sundays only, 8am-1pm); if you don't want to buy, go for the spectacle. London's three most popular markets are its three biggest, selling anything and everything. Best known is **Portobello Road**, W11, which is open all week in some form, but it buzzes most on Friday and Saturday: cool clothes, a pound of oranges, a Louis XV chair. **Camden Market** (Camden, NW1: daily, from 10am, best at weekends), is huge, comprises five markets in all, and is one of London's top five tourist destinations; if you want that pair of 1952-Levi XXs, the Stables Market, fun and adventurous, is the place to come. Finally, **Brick Lane**, E1 (Sundays only, 8am-1pm) is one of the few magnets that manages to attract lazy North, South or West Londoners over to the East End. It is fantastic, a great scene,

London's most interesting market (even if you don't buy a thing), a perfect Sunday morning experience. While you're here, stop for one of its legendary curries; this is the place to eat Indian food in London.

Making the most of London

Green spaces

The cleverest of Londoners fall ill and have to stay off work only in summer, and only when the sun's out. You will often find them sprawled out in their nearest park bravely recovering. There are hundreds of small parks, gardens and cemeteries all over London, and you are more likely to chance upon them if you walk, or cycle, around. Ask your hosts and they should be able to point you in the direction of the local secret. The following are the bigger places you might like to visit, ill or not.

Central

Hyde Park, bang in the middle of town, for bike-riding, kite-flying, horse-riding, deckchair-sleeping, people-watching, pleasure-boating, picnicking, on-line skating, even swimming in the Serpentine Lake. Check out the spectacular water gardens at the Lancaster Gate entrance. **Kensington Gardens** forms the western side of the park and is where you'll find the Princess Diana Memorial Garden, and the statue of Peter Pan. You can walk all the way from Notting Hill to Parliament Square (about three

miles) through Kensington Gardens, Hyde Park, **Green Park** and **St James's Park**. The Serpentine Gallery in Kensington Gardens is open all year round, 10am-6pm, and admission is free. **Speaker's Corner** (Cumberland Gate, Marble Arch, W1; Sunday mornings) is a must for those in search of an argument; just bring your soapbox and you are free to say whatever you want. Alternatively, come to listen (and laugh).

North

Regent's Park may house London Zoo, but **Hampstead Heath** and **Primrose Hill** are the places to head for. Hampstead Heath is as wild as London gets. **Parliament Hill Fields** gives views all over London. There are ponds to bathe in, you can even fish. Bands play in summer

Making the most of London

on Sunday afternoons. You'll forget you're anywhere near a city, let alone in the middle of one. A perfect place, as good in bad  weather as in good. Primrose Hill is less touristy than its southern neighbour, Regent's Park, and more popular with locals for its views over London. **Highgate Cemetery** (Swain's Lane, N6), where Karl Marx is buried, is another glorious place, one not to be missed.

South-east

A day in **Greenwich Park** is a great day out, with the Royal Observatory gazing up to heaven from the top of its hill; Guy Fawkes's co-conspirators stood here in 1605 waiting to see the Houses of Parliament blow up. Henry VIII was born at Greenwich Palace and even though he took Hampton Court off Cardinal Wolsey's hands, Greenwich Palace remained his favourite residence; his daughters, Queens Mary and Elizabeth, were also born here. It is London's biggest park and you can avoid the traffic or tube by arriving by boat. Ferries run from Westminster Pier to Greenwich Pier every 40 minutes, all year round (first ferry 10.40am, last 3.20pm). It costs £6 one way, £7.50 return. If you have a travel card, you get a 33% discount. The journey takes about an hour.

South-west

Clapham Common hosts major events during the summer and is a favourite of South Londoners. It is not London's most beautiful green space – in winter it is positively bleak – but it gives Clapham a horizon; few districts in London have one of those. Down the hill from Clapham is the nicely old-fashioned **Battersea Park**, with bandstand, children's zoo, a pagoda by the Thames, rose gardens, boating pond – very popular with families on sunny Sunday afternoons. Further west is **Barnes Common**, another London gem, wild, and wildly beautiful. On weekends you may come across a cricket match as there are a couple of pitches where fattening forty-year-olds still act out the odd dream. A couple of miles south-west from Barnes is **Richmond Park**. If you visit only one park while in London, pick Richmond. It is London's biggest (though technically Richmond

Making the most of London

is not in London) and feels more like the middle of the country. Wild woods, an eight-mile walking, running and cycling perimeter track, ponds, plantations, woods and spinneys, a golf course, the wonderfully named Spankers Hill, and deer, of which there are many. An idyllic place. A little to the north of Richmond are **Kew Gardens** (the Royal Botanic Gardens at Kew, to give them their proper name: open 9.30am, close 4.30pm in winter, 7.30pm in summer; admission £5) – 300 acres of tremendous beauty. It is worth coming simply to visit

the huge Victorian greenhouses – absolute masterpieces – but Kew has one of everything, be it tree, plant or shrub. There are many different gardens (rose, azalea, palm, etc); it has the largest botanical collection in the world. Arrive by boat from Westminster Pier (April-September): the journey takes about one and a half hours.

The Thames: a tale of two cities

The Thames plays a strange role in present-day London life. It is not a river that binds a city, like the Seine in Paris or the Danube in Budapest. Its inhabitants do not criss-cross it ten times a day. In fact, the poor devils who live to its north hardly ever see it, and they venture across it only in times of pestilence and war. It is worth noting that North Londoners and South Londoners have wildly differing notions of their city and of its boundaries. Oddly enough, many North Londoners believe themselves to be South Londoners. They live in places like Chelsea or Victoria, or even Westminster, and have an 'S' for 'south' in their post code. This confuses them greatly, for they live north of the river. Now, whatever disinformation you hear while in London, herein lies the truth: South London starts south of the river. It must follow, therefore, that North London starts north of the river – in SW3, W6, EC4, wherever. The divide in London has always been 'north' against 'south', with tribes from each land being noticeably different from each other. South Londoners are better-travelled than their northern counterparts, more open and gregarious, generally more worldly. A recent scientific study has proved conclusively that South Londoners are substantially more intelligent than their backward cousins from the North. For their part, North Londoners see South Londoners as second-class

Making the most of London

citizens, peripheral figures, good-for-nothings, hardly Londoners at all. In return, South Londoners pity North Londoners and usually send them in the direction of France when they find them lost in Vauxhall, begging for directions. North Londoners experience great trauma south of the river and avoid it at all costs. It is for this reason that North Londoners expect their South London friends to meet them north of the river. South Londoners oblige; they would never see their friends if they did not. But when, in turn, they invite those friends south, they are met by nervous laughter, lame excuses, or blatant lies. This is London, a tale of two cities. As for the Thames, it just flows by mellifluously, ignoring the warring tribes, keeping the peace. It likes a little bit of green upon its banks, at least a path where Londoners can escape the roar of the city. Recently, the greed of property developers and local councils has seen its foreshore sold increasingly into bondage, a heinous act of betrayal for which those responsible should swing; from Westminster Bridge, where the Thames swirls, signalling its displeasure. But despite the unwelcome over-development of Thames frontage and the ever-dwindling length of its riverside path, and despite the fact that few Londoners profess much affection for their river, the Thames cuts

Making the most of London

through London with sublime indifference, revealing its beauty only to those who look kindly upon it, while remaining a haze of muddy brown to those who don't. People who come to London and do not make a connection with it miss a beat of London's heart. The most popular walk

these days is on the south side between Westminster Bridge and Bankside; concrete all the way, but very pretty and with plenty of diversions: the London Eye (the huge Ferris wheel), the bookstalls under Waterloo Bridge, the South Bank, Gabriel's Wharf for restaurants, the Oxo Tower for its view of the City, and finally Tate Modern. Here, the Millennium

Footbridge – the 'swaying' bridge that had to be closed, an event met with hoots of derisive laughter by Londoners – will take you across and directly up to St Paul's; a great Sunday stroll. Elsewhere, the Putney-Bridge/ Hammersmith-Bridge

loop is lovely, very wild on the south side (halfway along you can take a detour and visit the remarkable Wetland Centre). You can stick to the south side at Hammersmith Bridge and head on up to Barnes, then cross the railway bridge and come back down to Hammersmith, or keep going to Mortlake, Chiswick, Kew, Richmond. You can walk all the way, or ride bikes. It's about eight miles to Richmond and the south side really is prettier than the north, with pubs for sustenance on the way. Ducks and swans, oarsmen and fishermen, peace and quiet; don't miss it.

Making the most of London

London books and literature

Peter Ackroyd's *London: the Biography* is exquisite: 2000 years of vibrant, stinking, wicked London – a tour de force. The London Encyclopædia, edited by Ben Weinreb and Christopher Hibbert, is a good reference book; no London home should be without one. The diaries of John Evelyn and Samuel Pepys evoke and illuminate 17th-century London; *Boswell's London Journal* (1762-1763), edited by Frederick A. Pottle, does the same for 18th-century London. In literature, there tends to be a common assumption that Dickens secured the patent on describing London and it is perhaps for this reason that other writers have either steered clear of 'London as character', or simply not been noticed for it. Those that have successfully brought London to life include Trollope, Wodehouse and Graham Greene (*The End of the Affair*, *Ministry of Fear*), but the writer who owns London these days is Iain Sinclair; if you want to read contemporary fiction with London as more than a backdrop, he's your man. Last, but not least, Gerald Kersh, who remains inexplicably undiscovered. His 1957 novel *Fowlers End* is to London what John Fante's *Ask the Dust* is to LA, or John Kennedy Toole's *Confederacy of Dunces* is to New Orleans. London rings from every page: mad, bad and defiantly funny; a big comic novel.

Making the most of London

Finally… a tale from the East

For those of you who would like to practice your cockney rhyming slang, the following may prove useful. For the uninitiated, cockney rhyming slang is a variant language of rhyme in which a word such as 'stairs' becomes 'apple and pears', or 'suit' (of clothes) becomes 'whistle and flute'. Thus you get the sentence: 'There 'e was, coming down the apples and pears in his whistle and flute.' Often the phrase is shortened to the first word only, making it harder to understand: 'There 'e was, coming down the apples in his whistle.' The language originated in London's East End; to qualify as a cockney you need to be born within the sound of the Bow Bells, the church bells of St Mary-le-Bow. We will happily send a selection of our books to the first five readers who care to furnish us with a full translation of the following story.

" I 'ad a right bull with the trouble down the rub-a-dub last month. There I was having me Tommy Tucker in the Johnnie Horner when in she comes and says she wants a pony, says she's heard the artful dodger gave me the Burton that morning. Well, 'e 'ad, but I'd been down the airs and graces all day long and lost the lot on some old nag whose biscuits collapsed five furlongs from home. My skies were as empty as the one above me; I was all but boracic. I spin her some Daily Mail, but I'm all Jack Jones, not a china in the Mickey Mouse, and there she is, saying I'm an 'oly friar. I tell you, I thought she was having a Bushey for a moment, but she weren't – not my ol' carving knife. 'Tiddly wink?' I says, trying to placate her, what with all her flouncing. Not a word – she's gone Mutt. So I says 'take off your weasel, get yerself a needle, order yerself a nice piece of Lilian Gish and park your royal Khyber on a lion'. And what does she do? Smacks me with her Olivers! Well that's it. I'm up and off, out the Rory, in the la-di-dah and off up the frog. Only problem is I'm doing 60 when I pass the grasshoppers. Well, it's disco time, innit, the blues and twos in the rear view, and I'm in a right 'arvey Nichol. I get pulled over. Now, not only have I had four or

Making the most of London

five apple fritters, but the ol' tax disc ain't exactly what it should be. Next thing I know I'm in a flowery dell, peasy, it is, cause there ain't a burnt cinder in the place, with a couple of Glasgow Rangers, both of 'em tea leafs, who pen like French sewers and rabbit all night long. In the morning, no Bob Squash, not even a dig in the grave, so I'm 'ardly looking my best when I came face to face with the ol' bubble. '£500 fine or two weeks in the bucket,' he says. Well, there ain't no thought in it, is there; I wouldn't spend an Abergavenny to save me from two weeks' bird. A nice little break, I thought, a bit of a reunion, and so it was: three meals a day and a couple of china plates. But when I get out, I can't Adam-and-Eve it; the Duchess of Fife has scarpa'd up north, gone to see her skin and blister, and, what's more, she ain't coming back. I was delirious; that Conan Doyle on her Chevy Chase was getting the better of me, I tell you. Last week I found myself a nice little cuddle and kiss. You should see her bacons; tall as the Eiffel Tower they are – works of art. Came home last night and found her darning me almonds. Soon as I can, I'll get cash and carried again. Then we can all get back down the rub-a-dub and have ourselves a nice little knees-up."

Quick reference indices

These listings are guidelines only. Please, when booking, check any details which are important to you.

WHEELCHAIR-FRIENDLY

Places with facilities for people in wheelchairs.

50 • Imperial College

58 • The Beaufort

64 • The Goring

65 • The Dorchester

LIMITED MOBILITY

Places that are accessible for people of limited mobility.

62 • Basil Street Hotel

68 • 22 Jermyn Street

76 • The Academy, The Bloomsbury Town House

WALKS

Places where beautiful walks can be reached within five minutes.

1 • Rival

3 • 57 Breakspears Road

4 • Shepherd's

5 • 24 Fox Hill

6 • 34 Ambleside Avenue

8 • 108 Streathbourne Road

10 • 119 Knatchbull Road

12 • 22 Northbourne Road

13 • 20 St Philip Street

14 • Worfield Street

15 • Paddock Lodge

16 • 147 Petersham Road

17 • Doughty Cottage

18 • Chalon House

19 • 131 Queens Road

20 • The Victoria

22 • 1 Charlotte Road

23 • 11 Queen Anne's Grove

25 • 31 Rowan Road

27 • Holland Road

29 • Portobello Hotel

31 • Miller's

32 • Pembroke Square

45 • 6 Oakfield Street

46 • Old Church Street

49 • 22 Hyde Park Gate

50 • Imperial College London

56 • Searcy's Roof Garden Bedrooms

57 • Parkes Hotel

59 • 37 Trevor Square

61 • L'Hotel

62 • Basil Street Hotel

63 • 16 William Mews

65 • The Dorchester

66 • Athenæum Hotel and Apartments

67 • The Stafford

68 • 22 Jermyn Street

69 • Hyde Park Garden Mews

70 • Norfolk Crescent

71 • The Colonnade, The Little Venice Town House

72 • 22 York Street

73 • Number Ten

80 • La Gaffe

81 • Hampstead Village Guest House

82 • 30 King Henry's Road

83 • 78 Albert Street

84 • 66 Camden Square

Quick reference indices

GOOD FOR SINGLES

Places that have good value rooms for singles.

2 • 113 Pepys Road

3 • 57 Breakspears Road

4 • Shepherd's

5 • 24 Fox Hill

6 • 34 Ambleside Avenue

8 • 108 Streathbourne Road

10 • 119 Knatchbull Road

11 • 8 Macaulay Road

16 • 147 Petersham Road

22 • 1 Charlotte Road

28 • 101 Abbotsbury Road

35 • Hartismere Road

36 • 8 Hartismere Road

37 • 29 Winchendon Road

40 • 34 Wandsworth Bridge Road

41 • 30 Stokenchurch Street

45 • 6 Oakfield Street

50 • Imperial College London

77 • University College, London

83 • 78 Albert Street

84 • 66 Camden Square

85 • 4 Highbury Terrace

INTERNET CONNECTIONS

Places where bedrooms have telephone sockets for modem connections.

5 • 24 Fox Hill

20 • The Victoria

26 • Addison Gardens

27 • Holland Road

29 • Portobello Hotel

30 • Portobello Gold

31 • Miller's

32 • Pembroke Square

33 • Amsterdam Hotel

34 • Twenty Nevern Square

38 • Crondace Road

43 • Barclay Road

44 • Britannia Road

46 • Old Church Street

47 • Elm Park Gardens

48 • Aster House

53 • The Sloane Hotel

57 • Parkes Hotel

58 • The Beaufort

59 • 37 Trevor Square

60 • 57 Pont Street

62 • Basil Street Hotel

64 • The Goring

65 • The Dorchester

66 • Athenæum Hotel and Apartments

67 • The Stafford

68 • 22 Jermyn Street

69 • Hyde Park Garden Mews

70 • Norfolk Crescent

71 • The Colonnade, The Little Venice Town House

72 • 22 York Street

74 • 23 Greengarden House

75 • myhotel Bloomsbury

76 • The Academy, The Bloomsbury Town House

81 • Hampstead Village Guest House

Quick reference indices

CHILD-FRIENDLY

Places where owners welcome children of any age – but do discuss any special needs: cots and highchairs may not be available.

1 • Rival

2 • 113 Pepys Road

5 • 24 Fox Hill

6 • 34 Ambleside Avenue

7 • 38 Killieser Avenue

9 • The Coach House

10 • 119 Knatchbull Road

11 • 8 Macaulay Road

14 • Worfield Street

19 • 131 Queens Road

20 • The Victoria

24 • 7 Emlyn Road

25 • 31 Rowan Road

26 • Addison Gardens

27 • Holland Road

29 • Portobello Hotel

30 • Portobello Gold

31 • Miller's

33 • Amsterdam Hotel

37 • 29 Winchendon Road

38 • Crondace Road

41 • 30 Stokenchurch Street

44 • Britannia Road

45 • 6 Oakfield Street

46 • Old Church Street

48 • Aster House

50 • Imperial College London

53 • The Sloane Hotel

54 • The London Outpost

57 • Parkes Hotel

58 • The Beaufort

60 • 57 Pont Street

61 • L'Hotel

62 • Basil Street Hotel

64 • The Goring

65 • The Dorchester

66 • Athenæum Hotel and Apartments

67 • The Stafford

68 • 22 Jermyn Street

70 • Norfolk Crescent

71 • The Colonnade, The Little Venice Town House

72 • 22 York Street

73 • Number Ten

74 • 23 Greengarden House

75 • myhotel Bloomsbury

76 • The Academy, The Bloomsbury Town House

77 • University College, London

78 • The Jenkins Hotel

80 • La Gaffe

81 • Hampstead Village Guest House

82 • 30 King Henry's Road

83 • 78 Albert Street

85 • 4 Highbury Terrace

GARDEN – PATIO

Places that have gardens or patios where guests can sit.

3 • 57 Breakspears Road

5 • 24 Fox Hill

Quick reference indices

6 • 34 Ambleside Avenue

7 • 38 Killieser Avenue

8 • 108 Streathbourne Road

11 • 8 Macaulay Road

12 • 22 Northbourne Road

13 • 20 St Philip Street

15 • Paddock Lodge

17 • Doughty Cottage

18 • Chalon House

21 • Leyden House

27 • Holland Road

37 • 29 Winchendon Road

42 • 8 Parthenia Road

48 • Aster House

50 • Imperial College London

54 • The London Outpost

56 • Searcy's Roof Garden
Bedrooms

71 • The Colonnade, The Little
Venice Town House

75 • myhotel Bloomsbury

76 • The Academy, The
Bloomsbury Town House

84 • 66 Camden Square

PETS WELCOME

Places with owners who are happy
for you to bring your pet.

4 • Shepherd's

23 • 11 Queen Anne's Grove

25 • 31 Rowan Road

27 • Holland Road

29 • Portobello Hotel

30 • Portobello Gold

36 • 8 Hartismere Road

44 • Britannia Road

68 • 22 Jermyn Street

75 • myhotel Bloomsbury

VEGETARIAN

Places that cater for vegetarians,
with advance warning. All hosts
can cater for vegetarians at
breakfast.

1 • Rival

3 • 57 Breakspears Road

4 • Shepherd's

16 • 147 Petersham Road

18 • Chalon House

19 • 131 Queens Road

20 • The Victoria

22 • 1 Charlotte Road

30 • Portobello Gold

50 • Imperial College London

64 • The Goring

75 • myhotel Bloomsbury

80 • La Gaffe

81 • Hampstead Village
Guest House

MEALS

Places that serve lunch and/or
dinner on the premises.

2 • 113 Pepys Road

4 • Shepherd's

5 • 24 Fox Hill

7 • 38 Killieser Avenue

8 • 108 Streathbourne Road

9 • The Coach House

Quick reference indices

15 • Paddock Lodge

19 • 131 Queens Road

20 • The Victoria

29 • Portobello Hotel

30 • Portobello Gold

34 • Twenty Nevern Square

36 • 8 Hartismere Road

50 • Imperial College London

30 • Portobello Gold

61 • L'Hotel

62 • Basil Street Hotel

64 • The Goring

65 • The Dorchester

66 • Athenæum Hotel and Apartments

67 • The Stafford

71 • The Colonnade, The Little Venice Town House

75 • myhotel Bloomsbury

79 • The Generator

80 • La Gaffe

ROOMS UNDER £70

Places that offer a double room based on two people sharing for under £70 a night.

6 • 34 Ambleside Avenue

8 • 108 Streathbourne Road

10 • 119 Knatchbull Road

14 • Worfield Street

16 • 147 Petersham Road

23 • 11 Queen Anne's Grove

30 • Portobello Gold

34 • Wandsworth Bridge Road

41 • 30 Stokenchurch Street

45 • 6 Oakfield Street

50 • Imperial College London

77 • University College London

79 • The Generator

85 • 4 Highbury Terrace

What is Alastair Sawday Publishing?

A dozen or more of us work in two converted barns on a farm near Bristol, close enough to the city for a bicycle ride and far enough for a silence broken only by horses and the occasional passage of a tractor. Some editors work in the countries they write about, others work from the UK but are based outside the office. We enjoy each other's company, celebrate every event possible, and work in an easy-going but committed environment.

These books owe their style and mood to Alastair's miscellaneous career and his interest in the community and the environment. He has taught overseas, worked with refugees, run development projects abroad, founded a travel company and several environmental organisations – many of which have flourished. There has been a slightly mad streak evident throughout, not least in his driving of a waste-paper-collection lorry for a year, the manning of stalls at impoverished jumble sales and the pursuit of causes long before they were considered sane.

Back to the travel company: trying to take his clients to eat and sleep in places that were not owned by corporations and assorted bandits he found dozens of very special places in France – farms, châteaux etc – a list that grew into the first book, *French Bed and Breakfast*. It was a celebration of 'real' places to stay and the remarkable people who run them.

The publishing company is based on the unexpected success of that first and rather whimsical French book. It started as a mild crusade, and there it stays – full of 'attitude', and the more appealing for it. For we still celebrate the unusual, the beautiful, the individual. We are passionate about rejecting the banal, the ugly, the pompous and the indifferent and we are passionate too, about promoting the use of 'real' food. Alastair is a trustee of the Soil Association and keen to promote organic growing and consuming by owners and visitors.

It is a source of deep pleasure to us to have learned that there are many thousands of people who share our views. We are by no means alone in trumpeting the virtues of standing up to the destructive uniformity of so much of our culture.

We are building a company in which people and values matter. We love to hear of new friendships between those in the book and those using it, and to know that there are many people – among them farmers – who have been enabled to pursue their lives thanks to the extra income the book brings them.

The Little Earth Book – 2nd Edition

The Little Earth Book
2nd Edition

'Only dead fish float with the current;
live fish swim against it'.

A fascinating read. The earth is now desperately vulnerable; so are we. Original, stimulating mini-essays about what is going wrong with our planet, and about the greatest challenge of our century: how to save the Earth for us all. It is pithy, yet intellectually credible, well-referenced, wry yet deadly serious.

Alastair Sawday, the publisher, is also an environmentalist. For over 25 years he has campaigned, not only against the worst excesses of modern tourism and its hotels, but against environmental 'looniness' of other kinds. He has fought for systems and policies that might enable our beautiful planet – simply – to survive. He founded and ran Avon Friends of the Earth, has run for Parliament, and has led numerous local campaigns. He is now a trustee of the Soil Association, experience upon which he draws in this remarkable book.

Researched and written by an eminent Bristol architect, James Bruges, *The Little Earth Book* is a clarion call to action, a mind-boggling collection of mini-essays on today's most important environmental concerns, from global warming and poisoned food to economic growth, Third World debt, genes and 'superbugs'. Undogmatic but sure-footed, the style is light, explaining complex issues with easy language, illustrations and cartoons. Ideas are developed chapter by chapter, yet each one stands alone. It is an easy browse.

The Little Earth Book provides hope, with new ideas and examples of people swimming against the current, of bold ideas that work in practice. It is a book as important as it is original. Learn about the issues and join the most important debate of this century.

Did you know.....

- If everyone adopted the Western lifestyle we would need five earths to support us?
- In 50 years the US has – with intensive pesticide use – doubled the amount of crops lost to pests?
- Environmental disasters have created more than 80 MILLION refugees?

www.littleearth.co.uk

Alastair Sawday's
Special Places to Stay series

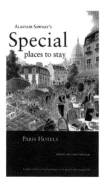

Alastair Sawday's
Special Places to Stay series

cestostay.com

Exchange rate table

£ Sterling	Euro	US $
5	8.07	7.32
10	16.15	14.64
20	32.31	29.29
30	48.46	43.93
40	64.61	58.57
50	80.79	73.22
60	96.95	87.86
70	113.11	102.50
80	129.27	117.14
90	145.43	131.79
100	161.59	146.43
150	242.38	219.65

Rates correct at time of going to press May 2002

Order Form UK

All these books are available in major bookshops or you may order them direct. Post and packaging are FREE.

	Price	No. copies
***Special Places to Stay:* London**		
Edition 1	£9.99	
***Special Places to Stay:* Portugal**		
Edition 1	£8.95	
***Special Places to Stay:* Spain**		
Edition 4	£11.95	
***Special Places to Stay:* Ireland**		
Edition 3	£10.95	
***Special Places to Stay:* Paris Hotels**		
Edition 3	£8.95	
***Special Places to Stay:* Garden Bed & Breakfast**		
Edition 1	£10.95	
***Special Places to Stay:* French Bed & Breakfast**		
Edition 7	£14.99	
***Special Places to Stay:* British Hotels, Inns and Other Places**		
Edition 3	£11.99	
***Special Places to Stay:* British Bed & Breakfast**		
Edition 6	£13.95	
***Special Places to Stay:* French Hotels, Inns and Other Places**		
Edition 2	£11.99	
***Special Places to Stay:* Italy**		
Edition 2	£11.95	
***Special Places to Stay:* French Holiday Homes**		
Edition 1	£11.99	
The Little Earth Book (edition 2)	£5.99	
Please make cheques payable to: **Alastair Sawday Publishing** **Total**		

Please send cheques to: Alastair Sawday Publishing, Home Farm Stables, Barrow Gurney, Bristol BS48 3RW. **For credit card orders call 01275 464891 or order directly from our web site www.specialplacestostay.com**

Name:

Address:

Postcode: LON1

Tel: Fax:

If you do not wish to receive mail from other companies, please tick the box ❏

Order Form USA

All these books are available at your local bookstore, or you may order direct. Allow two to three weeks for delivery.

Special Places to Stay: French Holiday Homes

Edition 1	$17.95	

Special Places to Stay: French Bed & Breakfast

Edition 8	$19.95	

Special Places to Stay: Portugal

Edition 1	$14.95	

Special Places to Stay: Ireland

Edition 3	$17.95	

Special Places to Stay: Spain

Edition 4	$19.95	

Special Places to Stay: Paris Hotels

Edition 3	$14.95	

Special Places to Stay: French Hotels, Inns and Other Places

Edition 2	$19.95	

Special Places to Stay: British Bed & Breakfast

Edition 7	$19.95	

Special Places to Stay: Garden Bed & Breakfast

Edition 1	$17.95	

Special Places to Stay: Italy

Edition 2	$17.95	

Special Places to Stay: British Hotels, Inns and Other Places

Edition 4	$17.95	

Shipping in the continental USA: $3.95 for one book, $4.95 for two books, $5.95 for three or more books. Outside continental USA, call (800) 243-0495 for prices. For delivery to AK, CA, CO, CT, FL, GA, IL, IN, KS, MI, MN, MO, NE, NM, NC, OK, SC, TN, TX, VA, and WA, please add appropriate sales tax.

Please make checks payable to: The Globe Pequot Press   **Total** [   ]

To order by phone with MasterCard or Visa: (800) 243-0495, 9am to 5pm EST; by fax: (800) 820-2329, 24 hours; through our web site: **www.globe-pequot.com**; or by mail: The Globe Pequot Press, P.O. Box 480, Guilford, CT 06437.

Name: _____ Date: _____

Address: _____

Town: _____

State: _____ Zip code: _____

Tel: _____ Fax: _____

Report Form

Comments on existing entries and new discoveries

If you have any comments on entries in this guide, please let us have them.
If you have a favourite house, hotel, inn or other new discovery, not just in
Britain, please let us know about it.

Book title: Entry no: Edition:

New recommendation   Country:

Name of property:

Address:

                                Postcode:

Tel:

Date of stay:

Comments:

From:

Address:

                                Postcode:

Tel:

Please send the completed form to: **Alastair Sawday Publishing,
Home Farm Stables, Barrow Gurney, Bristol BS48 3RW**
or go to **www.specialplacestostay.com** and click on contact.

Thank you.

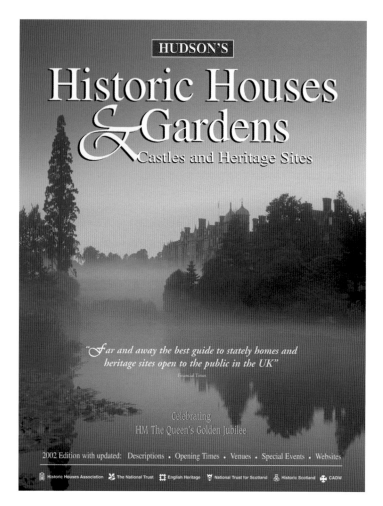

**Discover the best-selling, definitive
annual heritage guide to Britain's castles,
stately homes and gardens
open to the public.**

600 pages featuring 2000 properties with
more than 1500 colour photographs.
The essential heritage companion that is also a delight to dip into.

Index of Bed & Breakfasts

A

101 Abbotsbury Road	28
Addison Gardens	26
78 Albert Street	83
34 Ambleside Avenue	6

B

Barclay Road	43
3 Bradbourne Street	39
57 Breakspears Road	3
Britannia Road	44
20 Bywater Street	51

C

Chalon House	18
1 Charlotte Road	22
The Coach House	9
Crondace Road	38
66 Camden Square	84

D

Doughty Cottage	17

E

Elm Park Gardens	47
7 Emlyn Road	24

F

4 First Street	55
26 Florence Street	86
24 Fox Hill	5

G

The Generator	79

Index of Bed & Breakfasts

H

Hampstead Village Guest House	81
Hartismere Road	35
8 Hartismere Road	36
4 Highbury Terrace	85
Holland Road	27
Hyde Park Garden Mews	69
Hyde Park Gate	49

I

Imperial College London	50

K

38 Killieser Avenue	7
30 King Henry's Road	82
119 Knatchbull Road	10

L

Leyden House	21

M

8 Macaulay Road	11

N

Norfolk Crescent	70
22 Northbourne Road	12
Number Ninety-Six	52

O

6 Oakfield Street	45
Old Church Street	46

P

Paddock Lodge	15
8 Parthenia Road	42
Pembroke Square	32
113 Pepys Road	2
147 Petersham Road	16

Index of Bed & Breakfasts

Q

11 Queen Anne's Grove	23
131 Queens Road	19

R

Rival	1
31 Rowan Road	25

S

Shepherd's	4
20 St Philip Street	13
30 Stokenchurch Street	41
108 Streathbourne Road	8

T

37 Trevor Square	59

U

University College London	77

W

34 Wandsworth Bridge Road	40
16 William Mews	63
29 Winchendon Road	37
Worfield Street	14

Y

22 York Street	72

Index of Hotels

A

The Academy, The Bloomsbury Town House   76

Amsterdam Hotel   33

Aster House   48

Athenæum Hotel and Apartments   66

B

Basil Street Hotel   62

The Beaufort   58

C

The Colonnade, The Little Venice Town House   71

D

The Dorchester   65

G

23 Greengarden House   74

La Gaffe   80

The Goring   64

H

L'Hotel   61

I

Imperial College London   50

J

The Jenkins Hotel   78

22 Jermyn Street   68

L

The London Outpost   54

M

Miller's   31

myhotel Bloomsbury   75

Index of Hotels

N

Number Ten	73

P

Parkes Hotel	57
57 Pont Street	60
Portobello Gold	30
Portobello Hotel	29

S

Searcy's Roof Garden Bedrooms	56
The Sloane Hotel	53
The Stafford	67

T

Twenty Nevern Square	34

V

The Victoria	20

Explanation of symbols

Treat each one as a guide rather than a statement of fact and
check important points when booking:

 Children are positively welcomed, with no age restrictions,
but cots, highchairs etc are not necessarily available.

 Pets are welcome but may have to sleep in an outbuilding
or your car. Check when booking.

 Vegetarians catered for with advance warning. All hosts can cater
for vegetarians at breakfast.

 Most, but not necessarily all, ingredients are organic,
organically grown, home-grown or locally grown.

 Full and approved wheelchair facilities for at least one bedroom
and bathroom and access to all ground-floor common areas.

 Basic ground-floor access for people of limited mobility and at
least one bedroom and bathroom accessible without steps, but
not full facilities for wheelchair-users.

 No smoking anywhere in the house.

Smoking restrictions exist, usually, but not always, in the dining
room and some bedrooms. For full restrictions, check when
booking.

This house has pets of its own that live in the house: dog, cat,
duck, parrot...

The premises are licensed.

Payment by cash or cheques only.

 Within five minutes you can walk somewhere beautiful.

 Internet connections available.

Air-conditioning in bedrooms. It may be a centrally operated
system or individual apparatus.

The hotel has its own restaurant or a separately managed
restaurant on the premises.

Lift installed.